Who Can U Run To

Winning at Life!

Dr. Michelle J. Pullen

Unless otherwise indicated, all Scripture quotations are taken from the HOLY BIBLE., KING JAMES VERSION, NEW INTERNATIONAL VERSION, and NEW LIVING TRANSLATION VERSION.

WHO CAN U RUN TO

ISBN-13:978-0615956411
ISBN-10:0615956416

ABOUT THE BOOK

The issues of Life can either MAKE YOU or BREAK YOU. It's your decision on what you allow. Whatever life throws your way, you can't allow it to hinder you, nor frustrate you to the point of giving up. You should never give up nor faint when adversity comes your way. It does not matter who you are, you should have a little fight with in you to win. YOUR LIFE IS YOUR RESPONSIBILITY!

The favor God gave Joseph was greater than anything he had ever known. Joseph had been through the extreme; he had experienced the pit, slavery, and prison. But the depth of his past was an indication of the height of his future! Whatever you have been through in the past is the indication on how you will be blessed in the future. It's up to you to "GO" through without stopping. Leaving your past behind will bring you to your future blessings! Don't allow your "NOUN": persons, places, nor things, hinder you from moving into your destiny. When you move, those coming behind you can move. As long as you remain in one place, there is no space for others to embrace their race. You have occupied this space long enough, it's time to get up, and move! STOP HOLDING UP YOUR LIFE and STOP GETTING IN THE WAY OF THOSE WHO ARE TRYING TO START! Get out of the blocks and run. Staying in your lane will keep you from running in vain and exercising your gifts/talents will keep you in shape to move forward in your race. God will give you grace to embrace your race to help you keep your pace. So run at a pace that will help you win your race.

DEDICATION

This book is lovingly dedicated to the late Lessie "Lucille" Scott, the late Pauline Farnet Jones, and my parents, Eugene Pullen Jr. and Jessie L. Pullen who sacrificed that I may have the opportunity to LIVE! Thanks for being living examples, showing me how to love, teaching me how to pray, and how to keep my faith in GOD!

CONTENTS

ACKNOWLEDGMENTS

I owe gratitude to some awesome people who have been a great support system throughout this project. Thanks to Pa Pa and Wee Wee for giving me the tools of not giving up and go after my dreams. Thanks, Eulonda and Eugene III, for pushing me to the limits. Thanks Katonya for burning the midnight oil with me, it was worth the sacrifice. Thanks Rosemary, Alma "Juanita", Judy, and Geneva "Sis", for stepping in when I needed you the most. Thanks Chelsee', Chasmin, Jamarshea, Devin, Kari, Lonnie, D'Javion and Jamelia for keeping me moving forward! Thanks Paul, Tammy, Wayne Jr., Melodee, Christy, Tiffany, Adraina, Damien, Kelly, Rochelle, Joanie, Jackii, Terrance and Jarroid for being great team players. I also want to thank my mentors, teachers and motivators. But most importantly, thank all of you for believing in me and for praying without ceasing!

INTRODUCTION

WE ARE TROUBLED ON EVERY SIDE, YET NOT
DISTRESSED. WE ARE PERPLEXED BUT NOT IN
DESPAIR; PERSECUTED BUT NOT FORSAKEN,
CAST DOWN BUT NOT DESTROYED.
(2 Corinthians 4:8-9).

The issues of Life can either MAKE YOU or BREAK
YOU. It's your decision on what you allow. Whatever
life throws your way you can't allow it to hinder you,
nor frustrate you to the point of giving up.

"And let us not be weary in well doing; for in due
season we shall reap, if we faint not." (Galatians 6:9).

You should never give up nor faint when adversity
comes your way. It does not matter who you are, you
should have a little fight within you to win.

YOUR LIFE IS YOUR RESPONSIBILITY!

LIFE IS TO PRECIOUS at same time with LIFE COMES
PRESSURE.

When life's pressures try to knock you out, you have to
bob and weave at those punches. But if you get
blindsided by a blow of life that knock you down, you
can't stay down. You have to ARISE, STAND YOUR
GROUND, and PUNCH BACK. STOP ALLOWING
LIFE TO BULLY YOU. You have to make up in your
mind that you're going to get your life. No one or
anything should determine how you live. BE THE BEST

"U". DON'T STRIVE FOR BEING GOOD BUT STRIVE FOR BEING GREAT!!!

DON'T LOSE TIME BY WASTING TIME. You have to figure out what makes you FLOW so you can GO! Everyone has a different flow on how to GO about living their life and pursuing their life's passions. If you're not secure in the skin you're in, "U" can't win.

1

BEING SECURE IN THE SKIN YOU'RE IN

Being secure in the skin you're in will help you WIN. Remember, you can't depend on others to determine how you feel and how you live. That's your responsibility, not anyone else. So stop wanting others to make you feel secure about, who you are. You're too busy trying to get to know everyone else and don't even know who you are. Take timeout and get to know you.

You were born to win. When you were born, you were celebrated. The room was filled with expectation. The doctor, nurse, family, and friends were surrounding the room inside and out with balloons, teddy bears, cards, cigars, and etc. Phones were on standby ready to announce to the world that you have arrived. Smiles of happiness, heartbeats of love, and tears of joy magnified the atmosphere because "U" were about to enter this thing we call LIFE. Your first breath, breathed life into all those who were waiting for your arrival. It was a time of hope and new beginnings. LIGHTS, CAMERA and ACTION!!! The story of your life has begun... It started with "Once upon a time... but now you're in "In the between time..." Meaning the story of your life is still being written. What is being written of you is up to you. What would you want your life story to say about you? Remember, we all have a past, so we know how our life begins. There is no need to repeat our past. How would you feel about reading a book and every time you get to a certain chapter in the book it keeps repeating itself? Every time you get to a certain part in the book, and think it's about to be a breakthrough of something new, it goes right back to the beginning.

That's how most people are in their life. When you think they are ready to move forward, they go backwards and their life keeps repeating the same episodes over and over again. The next thing you know, their life has passed them by. It has literally "past" them by because they couldn't let go of their past. Twenty years of nothing, wasted because nothing was added nor accomplished to move them forward. How can someone live and stand still at same time? It's like walking with no steps or momentum to go forward. You're standing in the same place for twenty years.

There is no one holding you back but you. So stop blaming others for where you are in life. Others may have influenced you, but it's you who have the last say about what you do. It's your decision. You are where you are because of you. The decisions you are making in your life might be because of who you have become. Only you know the real you. Others only see what you have allowed them to see. Do you know why you behave the way you do? Do you know what pushes your buttons? You are the remote control to your life. No one should have your remote control. If they do, you are giving them access to push your buttons and determining how you live. If this happens, you have no control over your life and you're allowing them to dictate what you do and how you do it. They will have so much control over you that they don't necessarily have to be in your presence to control you. The reason being, you have allowed them in your innermost part; controlling your mind, taking over your thought process and not being able to function without their approval. They will have complete control on how you're living. People allow themselves to get into this position because they have lost their sense of direction. Then they start depending on others to help them relocate their position. Not realizing that the entire time, they have stopped being independent and responsible for their own life. They began depending on others to live their lives for them. When you put your life in someone else hands, you are forfeiting your true blessings. You are literally settling for less and not the best. Only you know what's best for you. In otherwise, what brings peace, joy and true happiness to you? Don't ever give your passion of living to someone else. If you do you're giving up your love and entrusting it to someone who may not have the same passion as you do.

2

ONCE UPON A TIME

Before we get to the now and in between time, let's start with where it all began, so you can learn and move forward. Most people stay in the beginning because they don't know how to move pass the past. You may have been hurt and can't forgive. It may not have been the happiest time in your life. Yet, you still want to relive those episodes. You may not realize that just because it made you happy in the past, it can hinder you from moving forward. Just because it made you happy then, doesn't mean it will make you happy now. For example, it could've been a past relationship; your first love or first marriage. No one ever made you feel the way they did. You thought it was going to last forever. Your first love is always the hardest to get over because it was your first time sharing everything: your trust, your heart, your innermost being, your thoughts, and your love. In other words, ALL of "U" because you thought this was it. You only had eyes for them. No one else mattered. Your black book, playas cards, and flirtatious ways were put away with. You found your soul mate. All was going great. The relationship was all you knew because you had become ONE, INSEPARABLE. But for whatever the reason may have been, you're no longer together. Whether it be divorce, separation, lost the compassion for one another, allowing others to interfere, or even death. Whatever the case may have been, you find yourself believing that no one else can make you happy nor make you feel as your past did. Living in the past hinders your now because you are still fixed on reliving it. Your Indication is, that you're still comparing everything to your past. For example, one might say, "In my last relationship they did it this way." HELLO, YOU ARE NOT IN YOUR PAST RELATIONSHIP. LET IT GO, ALREADY! It's up to you to let old things pass away and let all things become new. If you want to continue to truly LIVE in this LIFETIME, unclog your life and flow freely and continue to BECOME.

3

WORK-IN-PROGRESS

We all are a W-I-P aka Work-In-Progress. So continue to work in the progress of becoming new. You should not want to continue to wake up every day and repeat the same thing you did the day before. Remember, the movie "Ground Hog Day" starring the actor Bill Murray who played a weather man. As the weather man, he was reluctantly sent to cover a story about a weather forecasting groundhog. This was his fourth year on the story, and he makes no effort to hide his frustration. On awaking the 'following' day he discovers that it's Groundhog Day again, and again, and again. First, he uses this to his advantage, then comes the realization that he is doomed to spend the rest of eternity in the same place, seeing the same people and doing the same thing EVERY DAY. Get off your fanny and make it do what it do which is becoming the NEW U. No more past thinking but be transformed by the renewing of your mind. Your mind set has to change about what you think of yourself. How you think of yourself will help you determine what you want for yourself. If you feel like what you want for yourself is not enough. Why settle? You are FEARFULLY and WONDERFULLY MADE, A UNIQUE CREATION that is ONE OF A KIND, and there is NO ONE ELSE in this WORLD that is like you. Your DNA (Deoxyribonucleic Acid) is the result that there is only one you. You are SPECIAL and UNIQUE. And only you will have the responsibility to make sure you know that. So stop wanting others to make you feel secure about, who you are. You're too busy trying to get to know everyone else and don't even know who you are. Take timeout and get to know you. It's all about you. Once you know who you are it will be easy to understand what you will deal with, what makes you happy, what angers you, what saddens you, what makes you smile, and otherwise, what makes you tick.

Knowing who you are is beneficial to being in a relationship. The benefit is you will succeed if you know who you are then you will know what you want. You don't have to enter into the relationship trying to discover who you are. You don't have to depend on no one else defining who you are and telling you what you want. Once you know you, you will establish a firm foundation and you'll be secure of knowing you're not the negative names they say about you. You have already discovered that negative name calling doesn't become you because you are already indentified by your true INDENTIFICATION. So every time you take a true look at yourself, you know that you are BECOMING. You can't concern yourself with what people say or think about your past. The past is the past, so leave it in the past. Don't allow your past to hinder your BECOMING!

4

WINNING IN LIFE

"WINNING IN LIFE" is victorious living. Victorious living is knowing that you have the V-I-C-T-O-R-Y. Sometime it may not feel like you are winning, but just know, that by not giving up, gives you the VICTORY. "

We are troubled on every side, yet not distressed; we are perplexed, but not in despair; Persecuted, but not forsaken; cast down, but not destroyed; (Second Corinthians 4:8-9). But thanks be to God, which gives us the victory through our Lord Jesus Christ (First Corinthians 15:57).

No matter what may come your way, it doesn't mean life stops. It's up to you to keep the momentum. Divorce, death of a loved one, loss of a job, foreclosure on your home, repossession of a car, family in prison, drug addiction, student loans, no food, no drink, and your body has been taken over with lupus, AIDS, cancer, tuberculosis, fibromyalgia, shingles, rheumatoid arthritis, Parkinson, diabetes, brain tumor, etc., no support system to see you through. Be encouraged because Jesus said, "The thief cometh not, but to steal, and to kill, and to destroy: I am come that they might have life, and that they might have it more abundantly."(John 10:10). Living your life in Jesus Christ empowers you to defeat the enemy. When you confess with your mouth and believe in your heart that God raised Jesus from the dead, you shall be saved (Romans 10:9). For by grace are you saved through faith; and that not of yourself: it is a gift of God: (Ephesians 2:8).The Apostle Paul said, "For I delivered unto you first of all that which I also received, how that Christ died for our sins according to the scriptures; and that he was buried, and that he arose being three days in the tomb according to scriptures": (1Corinthians 15:3-4). In whom you also trusted, after that you heard the word of truth, the gospel of your salvation: in whom also after that you believed, you were sealed with that Holy Spirit of promise, (Ephesians 1:13). When you receive your salvation in Jesus Christ at that very moment you were sealed with His Spirit unto the day of redemption.

The Purpose of the Holy Spirit:

He convicts the world of sin, righteousness, and of judgment.

He transforms us in the sight of God.

He helps us to remember the word of God.

He helps us to lead a godly life.

He gives us spiritual gifts for the edification of believers.

He is our guarantee of eternal life with God.

He empowers us to be witnesses for our Lord Jesus Christ.

Acts1:8 "But you shall receive power, after the Holy Spirit is come upon you…."

Ephesians 3:20 "Now unto him that is able to do exceeding abundantly above all that we ask or think, according to the power that works in us,"

The Holy Spirit empowers us to overcome lives adversities and struggles. The anointing of the Holy Spirit destroys the yoke and removes burdens.

The Holy Spirit doesn't work alone; we have to ignite the fire through our faith.

But without faith it is impossible to please him: for he that come to God must believe that he is, and that he rewards them that diligently seek him. (Hebrews11:6).

"And Jesus answering said unto them, Have faith in God. For verily I say unto you, That whosoever shall say unto this mountain, Be thou removed, and be thou cast into sea; and shall not doubt in his heart, but shall believe that those things which he said shall come to pass; he shall have whatsoever he said. Therefore I say unto you, what things so ever you desire, when you pray, believe that you receive them, and you shall have them. (Mark 11:23-24).

Your unbelief will keep you from your breakthrough. Matthew 13:58 "And he did not many works there because of their unbelief."

You can't stagger at the promise of God through doubt and unbelief; but you have to be strong in faith. Just because it is impossible with men, but it is not with God: for with God all things are possible.

Jeremiah 32:27, "Behold, I am the Lord, the God of all flesh: is there anything too hard for me?"

It doesn't matter what you're going through, ignite the fire within you, through faith in God to carry you through. Just because it seems like nothing is happening, know that God's grace is sufficient and it will keep you until you receive your breakthrough. If you are still alive it is because of His Grace and Mercy. And each day you wake up it is God breathing life into you. But not only breathing life into you but turning your dead situation into life. You're being reconstructed to becoming new. I know it may be uncomfortable and even frustrating BUT GOD Is working it out for your GOOD because you love Him and are the called according to His Purpose. Hardships and adversities are preparation to root up, destroy, and tear down the old to rebuild something new. So change your attitude and mindset of whatever mountain (lupus, cancer, & etc...) that is blocking you. Look at it is coming down and being removed. Just like a reckon ball and dynamite they use to demolish old buildings. The fear that is tormenting you is about to be blown out of you like dynamite. When the explosion occurs you will be like the three Hebrew boys who were in the Bible, in the Book of Daniel Chapter Three; who will be discussed later. They were thrown into a fiery furnace, but they came out without a stench. Coming out without a stench of what you're been through and looking Brand New! There is no secret of what God can do. If He did it for others, He can do it for "U"! My aunt and cousin, which are a mother and a son, were both diagnosed with cancer. They went through chemotherapy, radiation, and other treatments. These treatments made it difficult for them to function throughout the day because of the pain and drain. Even the medication made them weak. Too weak to eat and they couldn't even stand on their feet. At times they became isolated because they couldn't keep up with their daily routines. Isolated because of their appearance; once upon a time they had hair but now nothing left on their head for them even to brush. They both had to resort to wearing hats and wigs. Even the radiation from their treatments changed the coloration of their skin. Their bodies had gone from firmness to fragile. Even though their outward appearance was no longer the same, they both kept their heartbeat for God which was demonstrated through their faith. And it is because of their faith in God they are both cancer free; they both were made whole. Jeremiah 32:27 "Behold, I am the LORD, the GOD of all flesh: is there anything too hard for me?" What God can do for others, he is also able to do the same for you. There was a woman who had an issue of blood for twelve years, and had suffered many things of many physicians, and had spent all she had, and was nothing bettered, but grew worse. (Mark 5:25-26) When everything else fails, WHO CAN U RUN TO?   She also demonstrated how to obtain the healing power of God by the grace of Jesus

Christ through faith that produces healing. Her constant hemorrhage was a disaster Luke 8:43-48). It left her anemic, weak, breathless and hardly able to walk. Because she had no money she was no longer able to eat nourishing food to compensate for her loss of strength.

There was a difference between the woman with the issue of blood and Naaman the leper. Naaman wanted someone to come and heal him (Second Kings 5:11). But the woman with the issue of blood went looking for Jesus. She pressed through and overcame obstacles (Mark 5:27, Luke 8:45). She pressed through the crowd. She wouldn't take no for an answer. She fought the good fight of faith. She kept her focus on Jesus. She demonstrated her faith and confidence in Jesus by her determination. For she said, if I may touch but his clothes, his garment, or the border of his garment, I shall be whole (Mark 5:28, Matthew 9:21-22, Luke 8:44). For she kept saying, if I only touch His garments, I shall be restored to health. The woman with the issue of blood was using her faith. Jesus said, "If you have faith as a grain of mustard seed, you shall say...." (Matthew 17:20). Real faith believes what God has already done by grace through Christ Jesus. Real faith only appropriates what Jesus has already provided. In this woman's case, Jesus hadn't yet provided physical healing through his atoning work at Calvary (First Peter 2:24, Matthew 8:17, Isaiah 53:4-5, John 19:28-30, Romans 5:11).

For he had healed many; insomuch that they pressed upon him for to touch him, as many as had plagues (Mark 3:10). And the whole multitude sought to touch him: for there went virtue out of him, and healed them all (Luke 6:19). Wherever He entered, into villages, cities, or the country, they laid the sick in the marketplaces, and begged Him that they might just touch the hem of His garment. And as many as touched Him were made well (Mark 6:33). Jesus demonstrated over and over that he was both willingly and able to heal all. The woman's faith was only appropriating what Jesus was willingly to give. Faith is not something that you do but something that you believe Jesus will do. The Bible states, in Hebrews 11:1, Faith is the substances of things hoped for, the evidence of things not seen. Her faith filled her hope with faith that she will not grow worse. Jesus said in Mark 11:23, "whosoever shall believe that those things which he saith shall come to pass; he shall have whatsoever he saith".

When the woman with the issue of blood touched Jesus, she accessed the grace of Jesus Christ by her faith, her confidence in Jesus. By whom we have access by faith into this grace wherein we stand, and rejoice in hope of the glory of God (Romans 5:2). This woman had heard many wonderful truths about Jesus. She believed when she touched him, she would be whole. When she touched Jesus, the source of grace; she received grace for grace (John 1:16). The woman with the issue of blood simply believed Jesus and received power to be whole. Jesus is our source for eternal salvation, physical healing, deliverance, prosperity, and everything that you need. God wants you healed and he has provided many options for you to receive what Jesus has already provided. However, if you are a born-again believer, Jesus has already provided this grace to you. In Ephesians 2:7 say, "That in the ages to come he might show the exceeding riches of his grace in his kindness toward us through Christ Jesus. You are already complete in Jesus (Colossians 2:10). Jesus is already inside of you according to Romans 8:9-11 and Colossians 1:27. You don't have to press through a crowd to reach Jesus like this woman. This woman did because, Jesus had not yet died and provided the atonement for sin which causes disease but Romans 5:11 says, we also joy in God through our Lord Jesus Christ, by whom we have now received the atonement. Jesus has already accomplished our salvation, healing, prosperity, and deliverance and placed it in your born-again spirit, new creation. "Therefore if any man be in Christ, he is a new creature: old things are passed away; Behold, all things are become new (Second Corinthians 5:17). We are looking unto Jesus the Author and Finisher of our Faith. In John 19:30, Jesus said "it is finished". God has already done all that he is ever going to do through Jesus Christ. Faith just appropriates what Jesus has already done.

5

PURPOSE DRIVING

Your Life is PURPOSE DRIVING.

The reason you're going through is because you have PURPOSE.

You still exist and have not been taken out because you are PURPOSE. Your existence is evident that you're in the plan of God.

Jeremiah 29:11, For I know the plans that I think toward you, said the Lord, plans of peace, and not of evil, to give you an expected end.

Jeremiah 1:5, Before I formed you in the belly I knew you; and before you came forth out of the womb I sanctified you, and I ordained you a prophet unto the nations.

As God knew Jeremiah, He also knows you. For as a man thinks in his heart so is he. You have to ask God as King David did in Psalms 51:10 to create in you a clean heart. You can't allow the past condemnation hinder your momentum forward. Don't be stuck in the **mess that is producing less and hindering you from giving your best.** Go get your Life. Remember, your life is a story being written by you and you're the only one that can write it. "The only letter of recommendation we need is you yourselves. Your lives are a letter written in our hearts; everyone can read it... (2 Corinthians 2:2).

What do you want your life to say about you? Would you like what you have accomplished so far or would you be embarrass for lack of achievement in your life? It's never too late to BECOME.

Just because your life may have started out rough doesn't mean your journey have to continue that way. To be honest, we all have a "ONCE UP ON A TIME..." Once up on a time being past tense. Your life story may have started there but it doesn't have to end there. There is no true end unless you believe in eternal life. But from this prospective, we're writing about life until it ends here on earth. From the day you were born until the day you die.

You can't allow your past to determine where you are today. I'm not saying your past can't motivate you to move forward but don't get stuck in a place where you've out grown. Know when it's time to let go and move. When you move let's not move to familiarity. Meaning you moved but you didn't move forward. You've moved physically but not mentally. In other words, all you did was change location and brought along the same baggage. Carrying the same baggage around all the time becomes a heavy load. All you are doing is continually piling on the mess. The more you pile on the heavier it becomes because nothing is thrown away. It's just like trash bags. The more trash you pile into the bag, it will expand and sooner or later it will burst. And when it burst it will become more trash. The very thing that was used to put trash in becomes trash. As the heart pumps, it sends

18

blood circulating throughout our body, ensuring that oxygen and nutrients are brought to organs and tissues and that harmful waste are carried away. We use the parts of our past that are beneficial to us, those parts that motivates us and encourages us to move us forward. It helps us get rid of the past that hinders us and clogs up our future. If it clogs up our future there is no hope of becoming anything and we will be like a dead man walking; hopeless and lifeless. There is nothing sadder than a person alive breathing the air in and out but breathless when it comes to living their life. Your life is in need of resuscitation. Resuscitation is to restore life. To restore life you can no longer be conformed to the past that's hindering you. Only you can identify what that is.

Identify your hindrance that's affecting your life. What happened in the past that's keeping you at a standstill? What past struggles are you fighting? What is keeping you from facing it head on? Is the past, too painful to deal with? Things that are left undone, if not destroyed, will continue to grow.

List of past hindrance:

Molestation

Rape

Prostitution (voluntary or against your will)

Left for dead

Sexual Abuse

Verbally Abuse

Physical Abused causing bodily harm

Kidnapped

Past hindrance could've been caused by friends, relatives, stranger, associates, neighbors, or was it someone you trusted that stole your innocence?

There is also other list of things that could've hindering you:

Lack of attention as a child

There was absent of a parent

No authority figure to teach you

Practically raised yourself

No support system

No one to talk to (No Voice)

Left Out and looked over (never included)

Loss of loved one/loss someone special

Divorce

And the list goes on but nevertheless does one outweigh the other because what may not affect one person may damage the other. Past hindrances can damage you to a place of escape. Most escape comes through drugs, alcohol, taking prescription meds to cope with depression and even taken meds to deal with anxiety and insomnia for sleepless nights. Most people escape through other people expecting them to be like the Calgon commercial, depending on something or substance to give them a way of escape. In the Calgon commercial the slogan was: "Calgon, take me away." This commercial was for Calgon bath and beauty products. In this advertisement, a woman wearing a fluffy pink robe is seen in a chaotic home scenario. As tension rises, she utters the slogan "Calgon, take me away!"

This is the reason most relationships fall apart, even to the part of divorce, because they are holding their significant other responsible for their happiness. Not knowing that true happiness comes within. *Covering up mess will lead to stress.* What's on the outside is not the photo image of what's going on, on the inside. One minute you can have a smile on your face and the next minute all hell is breaking loose. It becomes a war between the inside and outside. The inside want to break out but the outside is holding the inside back. It doesn't want it to reveal it's ugly self because the outside is afraid of being judged by others. Please understand people will talk about you if you're good or bad. You can't concern yourself with what they will say about you because this will keep you from your breakthrough. How can you trust someone else with your past issues if you don't trust yourself? You can't enter into a committed relationship without trust and communication. It starts with you. Clean the inside out before you commit. Please understand that you're not perfect. No one is but we take what we been through and learn from it and keep it moving. This is what is called maturing. Maturing is simply developing. You're no longer the same but growing into what is purposed. Remember, you are here on purpose but it's your decision if you want to live your life on purpose. You're important and much needed because you are gifted to do things others can't do. It's up to you to identify your gift and put it to use. Start with what you're passionate at doing. If something frustrates you to the point that it bothers you when it's not done properly, maybe it's meant for you to do. It may even take a while for you to figure it out, but don't get weary and give up on trying. Keep on pressing. If it's worth getting, it's worth the sacrifice. No Pain, No Gain!

In order to develop healthy relationships, you, yourself have to be healthy. Most people don't get along with others because they are damaged on the inside. Even those with anger problems come from what was stored within. Like any other treatment or therapy, you have to admit something is wrong. By admitting it doesn't mean you are the sole problem. In most cases, people hurt people because they were hurt. Some people find it hard to deal with past issues because they don't want to re-live the past hurt and pains. But in reality, if you haven't dealt with it, you are changing location but carrying the same baggage.

Having the same baggage means that when you thought you have left it on 9th street, the place where you grew up; in actuality you never left it but it goes with you wherever you go. It goes with you on your job, at church, grocery store, and even at night when you go to bed. You can't run from something that you haven't destroyed. The only way to rid of it is to deal with it. Then destroy it, by not allowing it to rule in you anymore. If you don't destroy it, it will destroy you. It can be like a disease that has entered you're body. It's quiet but deadly. Every once in a while it will arise and when it does it causes hurt and severe pain that's unbearable. It's more than a simple OUCH! The pain is beyond mental capacity. It will even make you feel that everyone is behaving in a negative matter toward you and in reality they're not. In your perception everyone is the enemy when it comes to you. Then you use the excuse no one understands. **You can't expect someone to understand your pain if you can't define your pain**. It's your responsibility to get help and admit something's wrong. You have to STOP where you are and do self-examination. If you keep getting the same results each time you're in the presence of different people, maybe it's you. You will not know until you stop blaming others. They have no idea, why you're behaving in such a matter. Stop the blame, throw away the bottle, put out the squares (cigarettes that is), and DETOX!!!!

DETOX is to get rid of the waste. As mentioned before, one of the reasons that the heart pumps blood is to get rid of the harmful waste that's inside of the body. Detoxification is removing toxins; to rid the body of poisonous substances; cleansing. Detoxification can improve your state of mind and give you clarity.

Third John verse 2 says, "Behold, I wish above all things that you prosper, be in good health even as your soul prosper."

What has polluted you, now have to be evicted. No eviction notice is necessary. If given warning of notice, the pollution within you will be trying to negotiate extended stay. All baggage has to be thrown out. So it won't try to hold on to anything because if it does, it will revamp itself and take control. Once all the baggage is out, you have to make sure nothing is left to torment you. Tear it down and rebuild.

6

UNDER RECONSTRUCTION

Being under reconstruction simply means you're a WIP (Work In Progress). As mentioned earlier, W-I-P means we are forever "Becoming".

Second Corinthians chapter 5 verse 17 says, Therefore if any man be in Christ, He is a new creature: old things are passed away; behold, all things are become new.

When you're becoming you can't keep doing the same thing because this will put you at a standstill in your life. Doing the same thing, gives you the same result. Instead of doing a 180 you're doing a 360. You're making a complete circle. A 360 will bring you back to the same place never moving you forward. A 180 will direct you in the opposite direction keeping you from going in circles and back to the same place. Stop going around that same mountain. It took the Israelites 40 years to move forward on what was only an eleven day journey in Deuteronomy 1:2-3. It shouldn't have to take 40 years for you to realize that you're at a standstill. It took God to interrupt the plan of the Israelites. God used his servant Moses to speak to the Israelites. Moses said, "You have dwelt long enough in this mount." As God used Moses, so is God using me to inform you that it's also time for "U" to GET UP and Move! No more excuses, why you can't. You're no longer in captivity of your past. No one is holding you hostage but "U". Set yourself free and be the person you suppose to be.

You've dreamed long enough. Now it's time to wake up and make your dreams a reality. **Real dreams come true, if you go ahead and be "U"**. Take a look at Joseph in the Bible in the book of Genesis and what all he had to go through just because he had a dream. Like Martin Luther King Jr. said "I HAVE A DREAM…" So should "U".

What have you been dreaming of doing?

What's stopping you from making your dreams a reality?

Is it fear?

Being Rejected?

Is it Lack of Confidence?

Don't know where to begin?

No Financial Support?

Don't let these things detour you of becoming and doing something GREAT. Remember, you're PURPOSED! SO YOU LIVE ON PURPOSE! You have to be purpose driven. You have to stay focus and stay in your lane. Don't allow others to get you off course. It's easy to get off course. You can't allow others to consume all your time, if it's not beneficial to you. You can easily get off course by simply helping someone with their dreams. Understand there is nothing wrong

26

with planting seed and helping others but you can't let it become your dream that you neglect "your" dream.

Song of Solomon 1:6 "….they made me the keeper of the vineyards; but mine own vineyard have I not kept."

You can become so caught up in doing things for other people that your own vineyard is neglected. You can have conviction and take responsibility for others, more often than you would like to admit, and get too busy caring for everyone else and neglecting your own dreams. If you're not careful you can end up buried in everyone's situations. This can put your dreams so far out of reach because you're too deep in others.

7

TOO DEEP TOO REACH

It's time to dig yourself out of that grave you have buried yourself in. Know when your season is up with that person. In the Book of Joshua, Chapter One, "The Lord told Joshua, that Moses my servant is dead; now therefore arise, go... Every place that the sole of your foot shall tread upon, that have I given you...There shall not any man be able to stand before you all the days of your life...so I will be with you: I will not fail you, nor will I forsake you. Be strong and of good courage...Only be strong and very courageous, that you may observe to do according to all the law...that you may prosper whither so ever you go. This book of law shall not depart out of your mouth; but you should meditate therein day and night, that you may observe to do according to all that is written therein: for then you shall make your way prosperous, and then you shall have good success. Have not I commanded you? Be strong and of good courage; be not afraid; neither be you dismayed: for the Lord your God is with you whithersoever you go."

It's ok to help but you can't stay. It's only a passing way to get you to. Most situations are not only you helping someone, but someone helping you. When you get what you need, keep it moving. Not to sound selfish or ungrateful, but what I'm saying is once you've learn how to do it yourself, it's no need to stay nor go back to it. For example, when we graduate high school we don't stay nor do we go back to where we started in elementary school. We keep it moving to higher education. NEXT! What we have learned, we make it work for us.

Proverbs 4:7 say, "Wisdom is the principal thing; therefore get wisdom: and with all thy getting get understanding.

Once you understand what you have learned and what life have been teaching you; now you can move on to the next. Understand every moment is a teachable one, if you allow yourself to be taught. Don't get so high that you think you know everything. You can be an expert in one area but clueless in another. For example, you can be a medical doctor and your expertise is operating on patients but clueless on how to do administrative work. Stay in your lane and stay on course. Don't try to do someone else's job. Do your own!

8

TEAMWORK

I know we just discussed about taking care of our own but doing our own also requires help from others. It's your turn to step up and become the leader. You have to learn how to lead from the position of a leader. Once the Lord told Joshua to go; Joshua transitioned from a follower to a leader. He took control and began to move forward. He used what he had at his disposal. He understood everything served a purpose. That's a part of teamwork. We function in a world where everything serves a purpose. Even cow manure serves a purpose.

A pile of cow manure is not the most beautiful thing to look at, nor does it smell very good. But despite its unappealing aroma and appearance, cow dung can actually be quite beneficial. Whether you are thinking about using cow manure in your personal garden or are simply interested in its effect on the environment. One of the most beneficial things about cow manure is that it serves as a fertilizer. Applying it to your soil directly can improve the overall quality of the soil. This improves the size, quality, taste and appearance of whatever you're planting. Manure can even improve very poor-quality soil, such as desert soil. Unlike many fertilizers, cow manure is completely organic. This provides a safer environment for animals and birds can be poisoned by harsh chemical fertilizers. In general, cow manure is much better for the environment. Cow manure helps the soil retain moisture. In doing so, it prevents the soil's natural nutrients from disappearing over time. Manure also balances the soil's pH level, which keeps the soil healthier for longer. Manure also gives off methane, a type of gas that can be harnessed and then used for electricity. Even the most unattractive thing as cow manure has purpose. So if cow manure serves that much purpose, what about your purpose? You're so important that Jesus said in Matthew chapter 6 verses 31-32 "Therefore take no thought, saying, What shall we eat? Or, What shall we drink? Or, Wherewithal shall we be clothed? ...for your heavenly Father knows that you have need of all these things."

Your job is to not worry or sweat about the small things but stay prepared for the greater purpose. Most people think just because they're doing something small or working on a job which is judged as mediocre, that it has no significance. Every position is necessary in order for our world to function. For instance, in the Body of Christ function according to First Corinthians Chapter 12 verses 14-26, says, "For the body is not one member, but many. If the foot shall say, Because I am not the hand, I am not of the body; is it therefore not of the body? And if the ear shall say, Because I am not the eye, I am not of the body: is it therefore not of the body? If the whole body were an eye, where were the hearing? If the whole were hearing, where were the smelling? But now are they many members every one of them in the body, as it hath pleased him. And if they were all one member, where were the body? But now are they many members, yet but one body. And the eye cannot say unto the hand, I have no need of you: nor

32

again the head to the feet, I have no need of you. Nay, much more those members of the body, which seem to be more feeble, are necessary: And those members of the body, which we think to be less honorable, upon these we bestow more abundant honor; and our uncomely parts have no need: but God had tempered the body together, having given more abundant honor to that part which lacked: That there should be no schism in the body; but that the members should have the same care one for another. And whether one member suffers, all the members suffer with it: or one member be honored, all the members rejoice with it."

Everyone is important and has a purpose in this life regardless of what it is. If you work in custodial services, as a maid, sanitarian, construction worker, plumber, lawn maintenance, administrative, secretary, musicians, city workers, postal workers, military armed forces, fireman, policeman, kitchen cook, waiter/server, teacher, delivery driver, truck driver, counselor, cashier, chaplain/preacher/pastor, author, artist, painter, engineer, cutter/sewer, athlete, coach, mother, father, aunt, uncle, cousin, sibling, caregiver, doctor, nurse, astronaut, student, sales personnel, architect, telemarketers, housekeepers, manufacture workers, farmers, business owners, entrepreneur, senator, congressman, governor, mayor and even the Chief Executive. No one on this list is better than the other because they all serve purpose. So whatever you do, don't count it as a down grade, just consider it a position to your upgrade. **Don't settle for less but continue to do your best**. And just because you accomplished one thing doesn't mean life stops. It continues. Even when the President's term is over from serving his/her country that doesn't mean he/she is retiring from life. It's only from that specific duty; they continue to live with purpose by making a difference.

Being a part of the team of life itself should make a difference in what you're doing. Knowing that you have purpose and that you are purpose is motivation enough. Because what you are doing is not only benefiting you but helping the world to function. Every member is vital.

You were put on this earth to perform a certain task that no one else can do. DNA syndrome!!! As you work toward your purpose you have to be careful not to get lost. Sometimes things happen in our lives to pull us away from the very thing we need to be doing. And most of the time, we may not even know that we've been pulled away. It's so important not to get involved in things that are distracting. You can spend the whole day doing something that has nothing to do with anything. It is time wasted that you could've been working toward your purpose. Alert! When you waste time doing nothing this can cause a setback and even a loss of direction. You were moving forward but wasting time caused you to lose interest in what you've been purposed to do. Once you lose interest or have a setback, it's hard to make a comeback. If you have fallen, you have to get back up. Achievers may fall down but they don't stay down. They get right back up. People may talk about you, put you down and even look over you but there is no reason to allow that to keep you from being "U". Let us look at King David in the Bible, 1 Samuel 16. Before David became King over

Israel, he was an unknown shepherd boy who was a
brave warrior that protected his sheep. His appearance
was ruddy but handsome. When God sent his servant
Samuel to look for the next king he sent him to David's
father Jesse to pick from his sons. Among the sons was
the young boy David who wasn't even considered
because of his appearance. He was looked over. "The
LORD does not look at the things people look at.
People look at the outward appearance, but the LORD
looks at the heart." (1 Samuel 16:7 NIV) "And he sent,
and brought him in. Now he was ruddy, and withal of
a beautiful countenance, and goodly to look to. And the
Lord said, Arise, anoint him: for this is he (1 Samuel
16:12 KJV). David wasn't perfect but God still used him
to accomplish great task. David had killed both lions
and bears (1 Samuel 17:36) and he also killed the giant
Philistine Goliath (1 Samuel 17:49-50). Your experience
is to prepare you and to develop you to be STRONG.
Fight back with your purpose. Don't leave your
purpose to address ignorance. When others know that
you're doing something good, they will try to interrupt
the plan that God has assigned for you. Separation is
the best policy when you're moving forward. You may
start to hear some of your family, friends, associates,
co-workers and others say that you are changing,
you're too busy to hang with us, and we barely see you
anymore. You began to separate yourself at work by
sitting in your car during lunch time. You're not even
returning phone calls nor replying to text messages.
Old things are passed away, all things are BECOMING
NEW! The new "U" is shunning the old "u". You don't
have time to do what you use to do because it's not

getting you anywhere. It's your decision to let the past, pass away. You can usher in your NOW which will make you BETTER and GREATER "U".

9

SEPARATION FOR PREPARATION

It is so important that you separate yourself from whatever "NOUN" that is holding you back. A noun is considered to be a person, place or thing. Don't allow your NOUN keep you from your NOW. It's never too late. You can start where you are. Don't allow your past situation, your age, your lack of education or your experiences hold you back. Use what you have to start. Use your creativity to begin your journey. Your purpose begins with you. Do an overall examination of your life; starting with ONCE UPON A TIME and continuing with where you are now. This will help you find a starting place.

To move forward you must step out of your comfort zone even when your mind and emotions are urging you not to.

"Be not conformed to this world, but ye transformed to the renewing of your mind…" (Romans 12:2)

10

OVERCOMING AND MOVING ON

Overcoming and moving on will help you get it done. Moving on is getting passed the last. You have to live in the present and not the past. Some people can't move on as mentioned before, because they can't get passed the past. Everything is based on or compared to what it used to be like. So when you have the mindset of the past that's just what it's going to be. When you are living in the past, you're now life will pass you by. Wondering where time went. Your mind has not been transformed from the past because you have conformed to it. If you enter into a relationship with someone, you can't operate under what the past relationship was. That's too much pressure on the next person. It doesn't matter if your past relationship was good or bad, you have to leave it in the past. Your expectation for your new relationship will come crumbling down because instead of starting a new beginning you're comparing it to the past. **It's important when you begin something new to make sure there is no past residue**. Just a little bit of the past will destroy and not last. Most new relationships end before it ever began because the last relationship never ended. Just because the two persons went their separate ways doesn't mean it was truly over emotionally. If the emotions are still there it will transfer over to the next person. This kind of transfer, in due time, can steal the joy out of your present relationship, if nothing is done about it. It's imperative to deal with it AS SOON AS IT

ARISES before it becomes THE END. Indications that may cause it to arise may be a disagreement, an argument, criticizing, judging, or even saying something about what the "ex" did. You have set the bar of high, expecting the person in your new relationship to be like and do as the "ex" once did. Anytime you compare and ask someone to do as the "ex" has done, you haven't let go. This is a clear indication that you're not moved on. The only person who's stopping you is "U". This brings it back full circle to "U". "U", have to make up in your mind that you want to change. So before "U" go and try to change others by pointing your finger and blaming them for your frustration and constipation, "U", need to take a look at your actions and how you're behaving. DRUMROLL....SURPRISE it's "U".

Once you realize the ball is in your court now it's time to make a move. For instance, if you're playing basketball and your teammate throws you the ball and you missed catching it, then it can either mean several things. Either you weren't paying attention so your hands wasn't prepared to receive the ball, you didn't hear the coach when they called the play, or you may have even been pushed out of position by the opposition. Whatever it may have been you missed a great opportunity to move the team forward. If you are working with someone, it becomes a team effort. It's not about what the other team has done. It's about what your team can become. Just think of the options you could have had if you would have caught the ball. When the ball was thrown to you the team was given you the opportunity to make decision concerning the game. The team trusted you with the ball at a pivotal time in the game. Most players never even get in the game and only time they touched the ball is in pregame warm up. Now you're in the game at the time where everything is entrusted to you to score and get the team the big "W", a WIN. This VICTORY is so crucial to moving on. It's up to you to decide what your next move will be. One thing you don't want to do is get a turnover and lose the opportunity. The ball is in your hand. You can't hesitate but you have to make a move. And whatever move you make, you can't be afraid. You have to be confident that it will work. Everyone is depending on you. The fans are standing on their feet; the coaches are looking with expectations and your teammates are cheering you on; "U can do it". The referees are looking closely and waiting for you to make a mistake so they can blow there whistle. The countdown has begun. The clock is ticking "10, 9 … You start to move forward as you dribble the ball; the opponent approaches you. Time is counting down …8, 7… You crossed dribble to avoid contact with the opponent as you move closer to the basket. As you enter the paint, crossing the free throw line, time is counting down … 6, 5… Your momentum has moved you forward allowing you to jump. You hear the people counting down … 4, 3, as you jumped you released the ball. As the ball rolled off your fingertips time is running out… 2, 1. Simultaneously, to the horn buzzing the ball went through the goal as the clock hit ZERO. When the fans, coaches, and teammates saw the outcome, they began to celebrate with great passion and emotions; tears, dancing, hugging and a whole lot of smiling. The OPPORTUNITY TO MOVE ON IS SWEET V-I-C-T-O-R-Y!!!!! You can have the same victory and moving forward in your life? You will also be celebrated because the weight from the pressure of the past will no longer hold you down, nor will it hinder your new relationship from moving forward. You can WIN AT LIFE with SWEET VICTORY.

I also had to overcome and move forward because my life story was at a standstill. Procrastination was a death blow to me moving forward. I realized it was not anyone else responsibility but my own to do something about it. At first, I didn't know it was at a standstill. Until it dawned on me that I wasn't getting the results I wanted. I was getting the same results. I didn't see a change at all. Even though I was trying to make an effort by staying busy but I wasn't achieving anything. It's not always good to be busy doing, if you're getting same results. It was a waste of time and it was stressful. Nothing is worth doing if it doesn't cause a change. If you want to know if you're changing, listen to what you're haters are saying. Who else will pay more attention to you then your enemies? When you hear your haters talk about you and say you have changed. This is an indication that you're no longer the same. The enemy doesn't want you to change. They want you at a standstill and slacking. They know **when you slack, you will lack.** They would love to see you hit rock bottom and to see you thrown to the lion's den as they did Daniel in the Bible leaving him to be demolished (Daniel Chapter 6).

11

JOSEPH DREAMED

Joseph wasn't thrown into the lion's den as they did Daniel but he was thrown into several things. The way Joseph was treated in the Bible, in the Book of Genesis, Chapters 37; 39 through 50, so are those of us who have dreams.

If you're not familiar with the story of Joseph, Joseph was the 11th son of Jacob. He was born to Jacob's favorite wife, Rachel in Paddan-Aram after she had been barren for seven years. At the age of 17, Joseph was a shepherd alongside his brothers. Jacob loved Joseph more than he loved his other sons. Joseph would report his brothers' misdeeds to his father and Jacob gave Joseph a "coat of many colors." The other brothers were jealous of Joseph and hated him. Joseph only further provoked this hatred when he told his brothers about two of his dreams. In the first, sheaves of wheat belonging to his brothers bowed to his own sheaf. In the second, the sun, moon, and 11 stars bowed to him.

One day, Jacob sent Joseph to Shechem to check on his brothers. Joseph went to Shechem and, when his brothers were not there, he followed them to Dothan. When the brothers saw him, they plotted to kill him and throw him into a pit. The oldest brother, Reuben, suggested that they merely throw Joseph into the pit, so he could secretly save him later. When Joseph approached, the brothers took his coat and threw him into the pit. They sat down to eat and saw a caravan of

Ishmaelite traders from Gilead in the distance. Judah came up with the idea to sell Joseph into slavery. Joseph was sold for 20 pieces of silver. The brothers then dipped his coat into the blood of a slaughtered goat and brought it back to their father, Jacob. Jacob recognized the coat and concluded that a beast had killed his son. He mourned for many days and was inconsolable.

Meanwhile, the traders took Joseph down to Egypt where Potiphar, an officer of Pharaoh, bought him. Joseph was successful there and Potiphar made Joseph his personal attendant, putting him in charge of the entire household.

Joseph was well built and handsome and after some time Potiphar's wife tried to seduce him. She approached Joseph day after day but he refused her each time, citing loyalty to Potiphar and to God. One day, Joseph came into the house to work. Potiphar's wife grabbed his garment and said have sex with me and he ran away leaving his garment in her hands. She then pretended that Joseph had tried to seduce her and slandered him first to her servants and then to her husband. Potiphar was furious and sent Joseph to a jail for the king's prisoners.

In prison, the chief jailor liked Joseph and put him in charge of all the other prisoners, including Pharaoh's butler and baker. One night both the butler and the baker had strange dreams. Joseph interpreted the dreams, saying that in three days the butler would be recalled to his former position while the baker would be killed. Sure enough, three days later, Pharaoh restored the butler to his job and killed the baker.

Joseph asked the butler to mention his name to Pharaoh in the hope that he would be freed, but the butler forgot about Joseph.

Two years later, Pharaoh himself had two dreams that his magicians could not interpret. The butler then remembered Joseph and told Pharaoh about him. Pharaoh sent for the 30-year-old Joseph. He appeared before Pharaoh and told him in the name of God that the dreams forecasted seven years of plentiful crops followed by seven years of famine. He advised Pharaoh to make a wise man commissioner over the land with overseers to gather and store food from the seven years of abundance to save for the years of scarcity. Joseph's prediction and advice pleased Pharaoh and he made Joseph his second-in-command. He gave Joseph his ring and dressed him in robes of linen with a gold chain around his neck. Pharaoh gave him the Egyptian name Zaphenath-paneah and found him a wife named Asenath, daughter of Poti-phera the priest of On.

Egypt gathered and stored enormous amounts of grain from each city. During these years, Asenath and Joseph had two sons. Joseph traveled throughout. The first, Joseph named Manasseh, meaning, "God has made me forget (nashani) completely my hardship and my parental home" (Genesis 41:51). He named the second son Ephraim, meaning, "God has made me fertile (hiprani) in the land of my affliction" (Genesis 41:52). After seven years, a famine spread throughout the world, and Egypt was the only country that had food. Joseph was in charge of rationing grain to the Egyptians and to all who came to Egypt.

The famine affected Canaan and Jacob sent his 10 oldest sons to Egypt to get food, keeping only Benjamin, Rachel's second son and Jacob's youngest child, at home out of concern for his safety. Joseph's brothers came and bowed to Joseph, who recognized them immediately but pretended they were strangers. He asked them where they were from and accused them of being spies. They denied his claim but he continued to speak harshly to them and interrogate them. They told him they had a younger brother at home. Joseph then locked them in the guardhouse for three days before commanding the brothers to go home and bring their youngest brother back with them to prove that they were telling the truth. The brothers spoke among themselves lamenting that they were being punished for what they had done to Joseph, who overheard them, turned away and wept, but then continued his act. He gave them grain and provisions for the journey, secretly returned their money and kept Simeon in jail pending their return.

The brothers returned to Canaan and told Jacob all that had happened in Egypt. They asked Jacob to send Benjamin down with them but he refused, "Joseph is no more and Simeon is no more, and now you would take away Benjamin" (Genesis 42:36). Even Reuben's offer that Jacob could kill Reuben's two sons if Benjamin did not return safely did not move Jacob. Eventually, they finished the rations from Egypt and the famine became so severe that Jacob no longer had a choice. Judah told Jacob to send Benjamin in his care and if Benjamin did not return, "I shall stand guilty before you forever" (Genesis 43:9). So Jacob sent the

46

brothers back to Egypt with Benjamin, along with a gift for Joseph and double the necessary money to repay the money that was returned to them.

When the brothers arrived, Joseph brought them to the entrance of his house and instructed his servant to prepare a meal. The brothers were scared and told Joseph they did not know how the money got back in their bags. Joseph replied that their God must have put it there because he received their payment. The brothers then went inside and waited for Joseph to come eat with them. When he returned, they gave him the gifts and bowed to him. He asked about their father, and they responded that he was well, and bowed a second time. He asked if Benjamin was their brother, and left the room, overcome with emotion after seeing his brother again. He then returned and ate and drank with his brothers, giving Benjamin more food than the others. He then instructed his servant to fill their brothers' bags with food, return each one's money a second time, and put his own silver goblet in Benjamin's bag.

As soon as the brothers left the city, Joseph's servant overtook them and accused them of stealing Joseph's goblet. He said that whoever had the goblet in his possession would be kept as a slave, while the others would go free. He searched their possessions and found the goblet in Benjamin's bag. All the brothers returned to the city and threw themselves on the ground before Joseph. Judah expressed their willingness to become Joseph's slave. Joseph answered that only the one in whose possession the goblet was found would become a slave. Judah then pleaded with

Joseph, telling him of Jacob's reluctance to send Benjamin and of his own responsibility for Benjamin. He told of the sorrow that would overtake Jacob if Benjamin did not return. At this point, Joseph could no longer control himself. He sent away all of his attendants began to cry loudly and revealed his true identity to his brothers.

Joseph's first query was about his father, but the brothers were too shocked to answer. He reassured them that it was God's providence that sent him to Egypt to ensure their survival during the famine, and he was not angry with them. He sent them back with instructions to tell Jacob what had become of Joseph and to bring Jacob and his household to the nearby town of Goshen where Joseph could care for them during the next five years of famine. He then embraced Benjamin, kissed all of his brothers and wept.

Pharaoh heard that Joseph's brothers had come and told them to bring their households to Egypt where he would give them the best of the land. Joseph gave each of them a wagon, provisions for the trip and a change of clothing. He gave Benjamin 300 pieces of silver and several changes of clothing. He also sent a large present back for his father.

At first Jacob did not believe that Joseph was alive. After he saw the wagons that Joseph sent, however, he realized it was true. Then Jacob, at age 130, set out for Goshen with the 70 members of his household. He sent Judah ahead of him so Joseph knew that his father was coming. Joseph went to meet him and they embraced and cried. Joseph told Pharaoh that his brothers and father had arrived. The brothers informed Pharaoh that they were shepherds and Pharaoh put them in charge of his livestock. They lived in the best part of Egypt, in Rameses, and Joseph provided them with bread.

As the famine continued, the Egyptians eventually ran out of money. They begged Joseph for food and he gave them bread in exchange for their animals. After a year, their animals were gone and Joseph made a new deal with the people. He gave those seed to plant on their farms and in exchange they gave Pharaoh One-fifth of their crops. He nationalized all farmland except that belonging to the priests, and turned the people into serfs.

After Jacob had lived in Egypt for 17 years, he called Joseph to him and made him swear that when Jacob died, Joseph would not bury him in Egypt, but would take him to the burial place of his fathers. Joseph swore to this. Soon after, Joseph was told that his father was sick. He brought his two sons to Jacob. Joseph fathered two of the twelve tribes of Israel: Ephraim and Manasseh. Jacob assured Joseph that he would consider Ephraim and Manasseh to be his sons just like Reuben and Simeon were when it came to the inheritance that God had promised Jacob's offspring. Jacob then blessed Ephraim and Manasseh. Although Manasseh was the first-born, Jacob put his right hand, the stronger hand, on Ephraim's head. When Joseph corrected him, Jacob said he did it on purpose and predicted that Ephraim would surpass Manasseh in greatness. Jacob told Joseph that he was about to die, but reassured him that God would be with him. He also assigned him an extra portion of his inheritance, a privilege usually given to the first-born.

Jacob blessed all of his sons, giving the longest blessing to Joseph. He instructed them to bury him in the cave of Machpelah and then he died. Joseph flung himself at his father, cried and kissed him. Joseph then ordered his physicians to embalm Jacob. The Egyptians mourned for 70 days. Joseph received permission to go to Canaan to bury Jacob. He took his brothers and his father's household, along with all of Pharaoh's officials and dignitaries, and left Egypt in a large group. When they came to Goren ha-Atad, he observed a seven-day mourning period. Joseph and his brothers then continued to the cave of Machpelah where they buried Jacob. They then returned to Egypt.

Once Jacob was dead, the brothers were scared that Joseph would take revenge on them for selling him. They sent a message to Joseph saying that before his death Jacob had instructed them to tell Joseph to forgive them. They then offered to be his slaves. Joseph reassured them, saying that God intended for Joseph to go down to Egypt to ensure the survival of many people, and Joseph would take care of them and their children. So Joseph, his brothers and his father's household remained in Egypt.

Joseph lived 110 years. He saw great-grandchildren from both his sons. Before he died, he told his brothers that God would one day bring them up from Egypt into the land that God promised their fathers. He made them swear to carry his bones out of Egypt into that land. Joseph died and was embalmed and put in a coffin in Egypt.

When the Jews eventually left Egypt, Moses carried out Joseph's bones. Joseph was buried in Shechem, on a piece of land that Jacob had previously bought. Joseph's two sons both became tribes in Israel and the northern Israelite kingdom is many times referred to as the "House of Joseph."

After reading the story of Joseph, you now know that he was his father Jacob's favorite son, who suffers at the hands of his brothers and became a slave in Egypt. He also being accused and imprisoned to dramatic rise in ruler ship of Egypt, and then delivers his family from famine to the land of blessings. What Joseph has been through is familiar to what others have gone through. You're not ignorant of the devices of your enemy. You know their job is to kill, steal and destroy your dreams. It's up to you to make sure he doesn't. Don't waste time trying to literally fight the enemy but you defeat the plan of the enemy by walking out your purpose and plan that God has strategically designed. So like Joseph, WHO CAN U RUN TO, when family turn their back on you, when they lie on you, when they throw you away and leave you for dead, when they sell you out to strangers, when they falsely accuse you, when they tell you they will not forget about you but soon they get amnesia, when they hate you and become jealous of you all because you have DREAMS.

12

INNOCENT

When Joseph told his dream to his family he wasn't expecting them to act in the manner in which they did, with hatred and jealousy. Well you know everyone is not going to be supportive of your dreams. Sometime the people you expect to be supportive will disappoint you. When those who you are close to, be it family, friends or significant others don't support you, it doesn't mean your dreams stop. Everyone is not always going to have your back. They are afraid of what others will say about them if they support you. Like Joseph brother Reuben, he didn't want their brothers to kill Joseph but he also didn't put a stop to it because he didn't want his brothers to hate him. So he suggested that they throw Joseph in a pit instead of shedding his blood. Reuben thinking, when his brothers weren't looking he will go and rescue Joseph. But when Reuben returned back to the pit, Joseph was gone because his brothers had sold him into slavery for twenty pieces of silver.

Psalm 27:10 says, "When my father and mother forsake me, then the Lord will take me up."

If you were forsaken by your family, parents gave you up for adoption and nor did your parents raise you due to personal issues, addictions, divorce or even them dying unexpectedly; don't think for one minute that makes you less of a person. Even if you were conceived by a one night stand or a booty call, people make mistakes but not God. Your biological parents, wasn't expecting to get pregnant with you but in the heat of the moment he didn't pull out and she didn't pull back. Semen spilt out and nine months later you were birthed out of an unplanned night of lust by two immature persons who were caught up in selfishness without thinking about the responsibility of the outcome. Regardless, of how you got here now you're here. Just because the biological parents conceived you do not mean they are the ones responsible in raising you. Irresponsible persons will raise irresponsible children. God loves you so that he assigned someone else to raise you because you have purpose to live and not die. What the enemy meant for your bad, God made it for your good. Once you begin to mature to the age of understanding and developing into a young adult the outcome of your life is determined by you. Yes, you may have not had some privileges as others did or you may have had to work harder due to the lack of support. This shouldn't cause you to complain, make excuses, nor become lazy as though the world owe you something. This should make you appreciate that God have thought enough of you that he gave you life. A life with a plan and giving you dreams to dream with a vision to get knowledge to bring to reality.

Everyone wasn't as fortunate as you. Due to an unplanned pregnancy and a decision made, they didn't have a chance to dream. Their dreams were aborted before they couldn't even have a chance to dream. They were victims to abortion because of a rape, a one night stand, promiscuous sex and even being a single parent or a married couple that decided not to have any more children. Whatever the case may have been, God knows. Who are we to judge? John 8:7-9, when they continued asking Jesus, and He said unto them, he that is without sin among you, let him first cast a stone at her. And again He stooped down, and wrote on the ground. When the accusers heard this, being convicted by their own conscience, they went out one by one, beginning at the older ones, even unto the last and only Jesus was left with the woman still standing there. God gives us free will. So when we do our will and not God's will then its God to judge us and not humans. Luke 6:37, "Judge not, and you shall not be judged: condemn not, and you shall not be condemned; forgive, and you will be forgiven". The only sin God will not forgive is blasphemy against the Holy Spirit (Matthew 12:31-32). If you had an abortion and you regret having it for whatever the reason; you were being pressured into it by your partner, you were a teenager at the time and you had no choice because your parents thought it was best for you and it will bring shame on the family, or your decision may have been influenced because you were told that it wasn't a baby but it was just a blob. But Jeremiah 1:5 says, "Before I formed you in the belly I knew you; and before you came forth out of the womb I sanctified you…" Ignorance is to ignore or hide from the truth. Whatever the case may have been it's done. You can't bring them back. Yes, it was wrong but you can't stay down too long because life goes on. You can't beat yourself up forever. The experience was a nightmare which torments you day and night.

Something that you wish no female would have to experience. Use your pain to gain. Turn a negative to a positive. You have to *take responsibility without condemnation.* This means to own up to what was done, yet not killing yourself with guilt. Romans 8:1 "There is therefore now no condemnation to them which are in Christ Jesus…" "If we confess our sins, God is faithful and just to forgive us our sins, and to cleanse us from all unrighteousness (First John 1:9). Use what you have been through to help others so they can have an opportunity to make the right choice. They need to know that life begins at conception. In the Book of Hosea 4:6 says, "My people are destroyed for a lack of knowledge…." You have a job, as well as, your enemies that are assigned to you. Their job is to destroy your dream by killing your vision. They know if they destroy your vision you will perish. In the Book of Proverbs 29:18 says, "Where there is no vision, the people perish… Once the vision is gone the dream can't be turned into reality because it will stop you from pursuing the knowledge you need to move forward.

Habakkuk 2:2-3 says, "And the Lord answered me, and said, Write the vision, and make it plain upon tables, that he may run that read it. For the vision is yet for an appointed time, but at the end it shall speak, and not lie: though it tarry, wait for it; because it will surely come, it will not tarry."

As Joseph stood by his dreams so should you. Joseph didn't allow temptation and the distractions from the world to forfeit his dreams. In the Book of

Genesis chapter 39 as mentioned earlier through your reading, Joseph was brought to Egypt after his brothers sold him and Potiphar, an officer of Pharaoh, captain of the guard bought Joseph. Potiphar saw that Joseph found favor with the Lord that he made him overseer over his house. As Joseph was working Potiphar's wife saw him and told him to come have sex with her but he refused and told her that he will not sin against God nor will he do wickedly to her husband. Joseph understood that no way of escape will make you play the role of a slave and just because it looks good doesn't mean it's good. Joseph refusing her, didn't stop her from trying. She was persistent because daily she tried to seduce him but he stood his ground and continued to decline her offer. Your enemy will try to wear you down until you give in but you have to continue and not be moved with temptations or distractions. Since Joseph didn't give in, she waited for the right opportunity to catch him alone. When all the other workers had deserted that's when she grabbed Joseph by his clothes and tried to force herself on him. Joseph didn't allow himself to get pulled in. He fled the scene leaving his clothes in her hand. While he ran away she had a strong grip on him, for him to leave his clothes behind. Like Joseph, you have to find a way to escape. You can't allow a feel good moment destroy what God has planned for you. You can't allow the grip of others pull you down, even if you have to leave your things behind. Leave it and RUN, RUN and DON'T LOOK BACK! In Genesis 19:26, Lot's wife looked back and she turned into a pillar of salt, looking back can kill you. Her looking back was evident and inclination to go back. If you look back, you may be tempted to go back and get those things you left behind which can be a trap to kill, steal and destroy you. Past things are not worth your life. Even when you haven't done anything wrong people will still accuse you of being guilty when they know you are INNOCENT. Have you ever been falsely accused by someone and the person that is accusing you, know that you are innocent. They may have accused you to get themselves off the hook because they would rather you, the innocent bystander, take the fall so they won't have too. They don't want to ruin their reputation because they are either well known or a modeled citizen in the community. WHO CAN U RUN TO when this happens to you? Will they believe you, a person that is not well known or that person that is respected by many? Just because you're not well known, nor in the public eye, this doesn't mean that they have the right to classify you as nobody. So don't allow those that are held to higher office then you intimidate your freedom of life to be who God has called you to be. As they looked over David in the Bible in First Samuel Chapter 16 verse 7b, "......; for the Lord see not as man see; for the man look on the outward appearance, but the Lord looks on the heart."

Joseph was INNOCENT but was found guilty because his master's wife lied on him and falsely accused him of rape. The only evidence she had was his clothes. These were the clothes she had forcefully torn off of him when she tried to seduce him. She wanted to bring this man down. She was angry because he didn't stay, so she can play and have it her way. After he got away from her, she realized she had his clothes then she cried with a loud voice. Loud enough that others heard and came acquiring. Once she got the attention of the other workers she told them that the slave they brought in tried to rape her. She used his status to downgrade him as a nobody. She told her husband, Potiphar the same story. Without a trial Joseph was found guilty for doing the honorable thing. Sometime doing the honorable thing is not popular and just because it's not popular doesn't mean you give in and compromise. Most people give in to the desires of the world because they figure there is no need of doing the right thing, if they're going to continue to accuse them of doing wrong. Instead of being innocent until proven guilty they find you guilty until proven innocent. Just because the other systems see it one way doesn't mean it's that way. We understand that no one is perfect but we also know that everyone is not guilty. Don't condemn others just to get your way.

After Potiphar had assumed that Joseph was guilty, he put him in prison. Once Joseph was in prison he found favor with the keeper of the prison. Like Joseph, you can't allow your circumstances deter you off the plan God has given you. Unlike, Samson in the Book of Judges 16, he didn't leave. Instead, he put himself in the position to fall when he fell for a prostitute named Delilah. She was a woman from the Valley of Sorek. It marked the beginning of his downfall and eventual demise. It didn't take long for the rich and powerful Philistine rulers to learn of the affair and immediately pay a visit to Delilah. Samson was Judge over Israel at the time and had been taking out great vengeance on the Philistines. Hoping to capture him, the Philistine leaders each offered Delilah eleven hundred pieces of silver to collaborate with them in a scheme to entice Samson and uncover the secret of his great strength. She became deceptive and used her powers of seduction to wear him down. He was infatuated with her, his lust for her blinded him to her lies and her true nature. He wanted so badly to believe she loved him, that he repeatedly fell for her deceptive ways. After the third attempt at luring out his secret, why didn't Samson catch on? By the fourth enticement, he crumbled. He gave in to temptation of lust and gave up his treasured gift, which was his physical strength. Samson's calling from birth was to begin the deliverance of Israel from Philistine oppression (see Judges 13:5). Having taken the Nazirite vow at birth, Samson had been set apart to God. As part of that vow, his hair was never to be cut. With her repeated requests, she finally divulged the crucial information. Samson told Delilah that his strength would leave him if a razor were to be used on his head. After hearing that, she cunningly crafted her plan with the Philistine rulers.

While Samson slept on her lap, Delilah called in a co-conspirator to shave off the seven braids of his hair. Subdued and weak, Samson was captured. Rather than killing him, the Philistines preferred to humiliate him by gouging out his eyes and subjecting him to hard labor in a Gaza prison. As he slaved at grinding grain, his hair began to grow, but the careless Philistines paid no attention. And in spite of his horrible failures and sins of great consequence, Samson's heart now turned to the Lord. He was humbled. He prayed to God—a first—and God answered.

During a pagan sacrificial ritual, the Philistines had gathered in Gaza to celebrate. As was their custom, they paraded their prized enemy prisoner into the temple to entertain the jeering crowds. Samson braced himself between the two central support pillars of the temple and pushed with all his might. Down came the temple, killing Samson and all of the people in it. Through his death, Samson destroyed more of his enemies in this one sacrificial act, than he had previously killed in all the battles of his life.

The story of Samson's life and his downfall with his love, Delilah, may seem like Samson wasted his life and that he was a failure. Yet even still, he accomplished his God assigned mission. He didn't go down without a fight. His weakness was turned to strength." This proves that God can use people of faith, no matter how imperfectly they live their lives.

Samson is no different than others, who have given themselves over to someone and was easily deceived because the truth became impossible to see. Samson lost sight of his calling from God and gave up his greatest gift, his amazing physical strength, to please the woman who had captured his affections. In the end it cost him his physical sight, his freedom, his dignity, and eventually his life. No doubt, as he sat in prison, eyeless and zapped of strength, Samson felt like a failure. At the end of his life, blind and humbled, Samson finally realized his utter dependence upon God. Amazing grace! He once was blind, but now could see. No matter how far you've fallen away from

God, no matter how big you've failed, it's never too late to humble yourself and turn over your dependence upon God. Ultimately, through his sacrificial death, Samson turned his miserable mistakes into VICTORY. Let Samson's example persuade you — it's never too late.

"And we know that all things work together for good to them that love God, to them who are the called according to His purpose." (Romans 8:28).

Life is BEAUTIFUL. Don't allow your mistakes, mishaps and downfalls change your perception of living. Get Up, Look Up and Keep Moving Forward!

13

DOING THE RIGHT THING WITHOUT COMPROMISE

Knowing that you have purpose will help you get through some tough times. Just imagine, if you were Joseph and were cast into prison for doing the right thing. As mentioned earlier, doing the right thing is not always popular but just know when you don't compromise something good will come out of it. In the Book of Daniel, Chapter Three, there were three Hebrew Boys. Their names were Shadrach, Meshach, and Abednego.

The three Hebrew boys are an encouragement to those of us who try our best to do right and what we believe. They stood together and didn't compromise even in the face of danger when King Nebuchadnezzar sent a decree throughout the land that mandated all of the people of the land to bow down and worship his golden image when the music was played. He commanded that all of his subjects bow down to his god because he desired that his god would be the god of the land. However, the three Hebrew boys didn't bow down instead they said, "Thou shall have no other God before me." They would not sell out to Nebuchadnezzar even though the king had blessed them with status of position and power. They would not give in even if it meant their lives and it was the popular thing to do. They had already determined for God I live and for God I'll die. And so when Nebuchadnezzar finally realized that these boys were serious, he became furious and out raged that he commanded them to be brought to him. When they came to him he said, "Is it true, O Shadrach, Meshach and Abednego, do not ye serve my gods, nor worship the golden image which I have set up? Now if you be that at what time you hear the sound of the cornet, flute, harp, sackbut, psaltery, and dulcimer, and all kinds of music, you fall down and worship the image which I have made; well: but if you worship not, you shall be cast the same hour into the midst of a burning fiery furnace; and who is that God that shall deliver you out of my hands? Shadrach, Meshach, Abednego, answered and said to the king, O Nebuchadnezzar, we are not careful to answer you in this matter. If it be so, our God whom we serve is able to deliver us from the burning fiery furnace, and he will deliver us out of your hand, O king. But if not, be it known unto thee, O King, that we will not serve your gods, nor worship the golden image which you had set up. King Nebuchadnezzar became full of fury and commanded that they should heat the furnace seven times more than it was. And the king also ordered for his strongest men to go and tie these three Hebrew boys up and take them to the fire. The Hebrew boys were bound in their coats, their hosen, and their hats, and their other garments, and was cast into the burning fiery furnace. Because the king command was so urgent that the fire in the furnace was exceeding hot, the flame of the fire killed those men that cast Shadrach, Meshach and Abednego in furnace. Even seeing the men killed by the flames didn't change the Hebrew boys mind. Not even the possibility of being burned into a crisp would make these boys give in to the king. Can you fathom a fire set seven times hotter than normal not devour anything placed in it? The normal temperature of fire is 650 degrees Celsius. So the Hebrew Boys was within a furnace that was 4550 degrees Celsius. That's 650 Celsius multiplied by 7. They walked out without a hair singed. Just the heat from a fire that hot could damage something, but these boys were in these violent flames and walked out without a blister. They were in the fire but the fire did not harm them. They were in the fire but the fire could not scorch them. They were in the fire and the fire was much worse than usual but they walked out of the fire in good health, good spirits, good attitudes, and with good looks. The smell of smoke did not even make itself present upon their clothes. They walked out of the fiery furnace as a representation of the power of God. And it is all attributed to God. God protected them. God proved himself to them. God proved to Nebuchadnezzar that no weapon formed against a child of the true and living God shall prosper. And most importantly, God showed everybody in the land that there is no other god but Him. And because of God they did not look like what they had been in. You may have been thrown into the hot flames in life and the God of Shadrach, Meshach, and Abednego has been there to help and protect you to endured life's fire. Some of you may have endured abusive relationships. Some may have endured racism, classism, and sexism. Some may have endured financial hardship. Some may have endured depression. And while you were in it sometimes it seemed as if it was seven times worse than usual. Your trials felt seven times harder. Your sickness felt seven times worse. Your worries seemed to last seven times longer. It should have killed you. It should have stressed you out. It should have had you in the psyche ward. But because of God's love, His care, His help, and His protection you have been in the fire, but you have not been consumed. You are living well. You smell good. You feel good. So, why did the fire not consume you while you were in the midst of flames that were seven times greater than normal?

The fire was not meant to consume you, but to refine you. The fire was also meant to destroy that which held you bound. When precious metals are found, they have to go through the fire as the means of their refining process. And what the fire does is it removes all of the impurities and unwanted materials in the precious metals so that when they come out they look smooth and polished and not burned and bruised. They came out as a representation of the fire's work. And the fire that you go through in life is not meant to destroy you. But it is meant to refine you. You were a precious metal. You were lost. You were hurt. You were distressed. You were just like Joseph, because the fire that was meant for evil God meant it unto good. The backstabbers have refined your gift of discernment. The struggles refined your faith. The hard time strengthen your heart. The trials worked your patience. When you were in the fire you found out that there was a **learning in the burning**. The refinery fire is where you learned, many are the afflictions of the righteous, but the Lord delivers them out of them all. The fire is where you learned, that when my mother and father forsake you the Lord will take you up. And when the

66

fire seemed like it was going to last forever you found out, they that wait upon the Lord shall renew their strength. They shall mount up on wings like eagles. They shall run and not be weary. They shall walk and not faint. The fire did not consume you, because it was meant to refine you WHEN YOU'RE STEADFAST and UNMOVABLE!

14

STEADFAST and UNMOVABLE

Therefore, my beloved brethren, be ye steadfast, unmoveable, always abounding in the work of the Lord, for as much as you know that your labor is not in vain in the Lord (First Corinthians 15:58).

Joseph was dutifully firm and unwavering because even when he was in prison he continued his journey to his purpose. He didn't allow being behind the prison walls destroy his dreams. As long as he could envision it; it was achievable. It's only when you lose sight of your vision that's when your dreams die. You can't allow your circumstances blind you of your sense of direction on where you're headed. This is where you can get stuck on one page of your life and the story will never be finished because it's incomplete. As long as you are living, your life should continue. You can be alive and not living, because you're stuck in a position of not forgiving. By this you allow others to control your life when you don't forgive. The reason being, you're still mad about what they did to you. What if Joseph didn't forgive? Joseph helped the chief butler and the baker. He told them the interpretation of their dreams. Regardless, of the outcome of the dream, Joseph asked the chief butler to remember him when he was released from prison. Joseph said I was stolen out of the land of the Hebrews: and here also have I done nothing that they should put me into prison (Genesis 40). When the chief butler was released and restored back to his position, he forgot about Joseph, the person who helped him out. Just imagine all that you've done for that person. You've bailed them out when they were in trouble. You were there when no one else cared. You sacrificed not having so they can have. And what did they do when they made it and no longer needed you. They FORGOT ALL ABOUT YOU. Now you need their help. All you ask for was for them to remember you. You didn't even ask for money. All you ask for was for them to put in a good word for you.

15

FORGIVE and FORGET

Joseph FORGAVE and FORGOT, instead of staying in not forgiving. Not forgiving someone will keep you stuck in one place and lose vision of everything else. Forgive and move on. Joseph forgot about what the butler didn't do. If he would've kept it in his memory, he might have became angry and bitter. Being in bitterness will turn into hatred. Hatred will cancel out love and the passion you have for life. There will be no room to dream because it will soon turn into nightmares. Bitterness will exalt to having a bad attitude and push you to the point of saying they forgot about me, $%$%#@$ them. Why stress and cry over spilt milk because it has no significance when it's wasted.

And let us not be weary in well doing; for in due season we shall reap, if we faint not. (Galatians 6:9)

Two years later after Joseph was forgotten in prison by the chief butler, Pharaoh had a dream. Pharaoh couldn't find anyone to interpret his dream. Now Joseph being 30 years of age, which 13th of his years was stolen. Since the age of 17 he's been a slave and in prison. It was good that Joseph forgave and forgot. If he hadn't, he probably would've been reluctant of interpreting dream for Pharaoh. And this would've hinder his dream and kept him in prison for the rest of his life.

16

MOVING FORWARD and UPWARDS

An innocent man was guilty because he was a dreamer. Nevertheless, his dreaming kept him and carried him through his process of moving forward and upwards. Being a dreamer this helped him to interpret dreams. Those dreams he interpret was his revelation and confirmation for his dreams coming to pass. Joseph interpreting Pharaoh's dreams is what moved him forward and upwards. Remember, Joseph advised Pharaoh to make a wise man commissioner over the land with overseers to gather and store food from the seven years of abundance to save for the years of scarcity. Joseph's prediction and advice pleased Pharaoh.

And Pharaoh said unto his servants, Can we find such a one as this is, a man in whom the Spirit of God is? (Genesis 41:38)

Where the Spirit of the Lord lead, He will bless indeed!

They didn't find anyone as wise as Joseph. Joseph went from living as a prisoner to second in command only behind Pharaoh. Pharaoh gave Joseph his ring and dressed him in robes of linen with a gold chain around his neck. And he made him to ride in the second chariot which he had; and they cried before him, Bow the knee: and he made a Hebrew slave now rule over Egypt a foreign country. Pharaoh gave him

73

the Egyptian name Zaphenath-paneah and found him a wife named Asenath, daughter of Poti-phera the priest of On.

17

SUPPORT SYSTEM

Joseph was not only raised to the position of authority but he also found a wife. "Whoso finds a wife finds a good thing, and obtained favor of the Lord."(Proverbs 18:22) Joseph is not alone anymore. Now he has a support system. Having a strong support system will help you alone the way. You don't have to do it all by yourself anymore because you have someone by your side to encourage you. The support system works when the both of you are equally yoke. Going in the same direction, on one accord and supporting each other dreams. Your support system are encouraging, not always complaining and tearing you down every chance they get. You can't allow someone in your life, that refuse to do what they need to do concerning their life and they won't change but they remain the same. **Don't allow someone else stress to stop your progress**. This individual will cause you to become a slave to their emotions and will pull you into unwanted stress which will cause you to stop your progress. Anytime you allow someone to interfere with your dreams it will distort your vision. Book of Proverbs 29:18 says, "Where there is no vision, the people perish. You need someone that will be there for you, as well as, you be there for them. It should not just be one sided, because the both of you have to support each other. When one is weak, the other one is strong and vice versa. Can't have the both of you being weak at same time and can't have the both of you overpowering one another at same time. The both of you have to know when to be supportive in any given situation.

In The gospel of Mark, Jesus sends the disciples out in twos. Jesus didn't send the 12 disciples out alone, he sent them out two by two. This isn't the first time in the Bible that we see God sending people out in pairs. It wasn't just Abraham that was told to leave his home, but Abraham and Sarah. When Moses was sent to the Israelites, God sent Aaron with him. When Jonathan attacks the philistines he takes his armor bearer with him. David, the king of Israel, had Nathan the prophet. Even Paul, who is credited with writing most of the letters in the New Testament, travelled with other apostles. Also in the Book of Judges chapter 4 there was Deborah and Barak:

In the time of the judges, Israel had drifted away from God, and the Canaanites oppressed them for 20 years. God called up Deborah, a wise and holy woman, to be a judge and prophetess over the Jews, the only female among the 12 judges. She was the wife of Lapidoth. She dwelt under the palm tree of Deborah between Ramah and Bethel in Mount Ephraim: and the children of Israel came up to her for judgment. She sent and called Barak, telling him God had commanded him to gather the tribes of Zebulun and Naphtali and go to Mount Tabor. Barak hesitated and said unto her, If thou wilt go with me, then I will go: but if thou wilt not go with me, then I will not go. Deborah agreed, but because of Barak's lack of faith in God, she told him credit for the victory would not go to him, but to a woman. And Deborah arose, and went with Barak to Kedesh. And Barak called Zebulun and Naphtali to Kedesh; and he went up with ten thousand men at his feet: and Deborah went up with him.

Barak led a force of 10,000 men, but Sisera, commander of King Jabin's Canaanite army, had the advantage, because Sisera had 900 iron chariots. In ancient warfare, chariots were like tanks: swift, intimidating and deadly. Deborah told Barak to advance because the Lord had gone before him. Barak and his men raced down Mount Tabor. God brought a massive rainstorm. The ground turned to mud, bogging down Sisera's chariots. The stream Kishon overflowed, sweeping many of the Canaanites away. The Bible says Barak and his men pursued. Not one of Israel's enemies was left alive.

Sisera, however, managed to escape. He ran to the tent of Jael, a Kenite woman. She took him in, gave him milk to drink, and had him lie down on a mat. When he slept, she took a tent stake and a hammer and drove the stake through Sisera's temples, killing him. Barak arrived. Jael showed him Sisera's corpse. Barak and the army eventually destroyed Jabin, king of the Canaanites. There was peace in Israel for 40 years. Barak defeated the Canaanite oppressor. He united the tribes of Israel for greater strength, commanding them with skill and daring. Barak recognized that Deborah's authority had been given to her by God, so he obeyed a woman, something rare in ancient times. He was a man of great courage and had faith that God would intervene on Israel's behalf.

Having a strong support system will help you fulfill your purpose. Someone there supporting you and looking out for your well-being. Your support system is not necessarily those who have been in your life a long time. Most of them will become new comers who have proved themselves of trustworthiness. There's a lot of good reason to go in groups of two or more. For one thing, safety was an issue. In Jesus' time it was dangerous to travel alone. The disciples were better able to look out for one another when they weren't alone. It's like the old adage that there's safety in numbers.

Sometimes life is discouraging. Having someone there to encourage us is sometimes the only thing that keeps us going. When we try to go at it alone, we are like the ember that gets pulled out of the fire. Pretty soon, we're just a cold discouraged piece of coal that has lost its fire and its passion. But when we are in partnership, we burn brighter and hotter and longer. We need the energy and passion of our partners in order to sustain long term goals.

Having a support system also keeps us accountable. It gives us accountability for both achieving our goals and for our personal growth. When Moses was gone too long on the mountain, Aaron gives into to the wishes of the people and makes an idol for the people to worship. It's only when Moses comes back down from the mountain that Aaron is called to account for his actions.

The same thing happens with us. When we are left to do things on our own, it's easy to stray from the path, and to stop short of our goals. We need to be accountable to someone who will tell us when we are going in the wrong direction, someone who will speak the truth to us even when it hurts.

What about David, when he got Bathsheba pregnant and then had Uriah, her husband killed. It was Nathan that called him out for his misconduct. Nathan helps David see that he had become more concerned with his own desires, than he had with the needs of Israel. Without Nathan, David wouldn't have been held accountable, who knows what else David would have done. Maybe David would have had anyone killed that he didn't like, or maybe he would have slowly taken foreign wives and lead Israel away from worship God alone.

While our transgressions are often not as big as David's were, we still stray from the life God intends us to live. We still have moments in life where we put our wants before the needs of those God have called us to serve. We need someone who will call us back to faithful living, who will keep us from wandering farther and farther off the path. So Jesus sent them out two by two.

We all have different gifts. No one person has every gift. We are connected with one another so we can compliment one another's gifts. We often talk about how we are called to different ministries. But we are also called to different roles within the same ministry.

None of us are perfect. No one person has every single spiritual gift there is. We need one another to balance each other out. We need each other, so one person can be full where the other person's gifts are sparse. So often in life we try to hide our bare spots, or try to get the sparse sections to grow so we can be everything ourselves. But that's not how God intends us to be. We're not supposed to do it alone.

So Jesus sent them out two by two. Who is it that Jesus is sending you with? Who is your partner in ministry? Who is God calling you to connect with?

Sometimes we are called to be in ministry with our spouse but if you're not married, you are still called to connect with someone. You can have partnership with someone that has different gifts than you do but passionate at things in common. As long as both persons gifts compliments one another. It should be someone who isn't afraid to tell you when you have messed up. Someone who isn't afraid to push you not to stop short of the goal God has set for you. Most importantly, it should be someone who encourages you, but knows when to speak words of encouragement to you. It should be someone who will walk beside you, but knows when to just walk with you in silence. And just as importantly, your partner should be someone for whom you can do all of these things. The partnership should be a mutual thing.

If you don't know who you should be connected, then pray about it. Don't just assume that God forgot about you. We need someone. It's not something we do alone. So pray about it. Ask God to help you discern who you are being called to be in partnership with.

18

KNOW YOUR POSITION and UTILIZE IT WISELY

In Joseph case, he partner with others along the way. He used his position of authority wisely. He didn't get selfish by making it all about him. He wasn't trying to exalt himself because God had already exalted him.

First Peter Chapter 5 verse 6 says, Humble yourselves therefore under the mighty hand of God, that he may exalt you in due time:

Joseph didn't take his position for granted neither did he mistreat the less fortunate. He was a blessing to those who came in contact with him because God had favored him. Regardless, of what he went through everyone was blessed and benefited through his presence. Remember, at 17 when Joseph was betrayed by his brothers. At first they wanted him dead but instead God intervene by using his brother Reuben to negotiate a deal with his other brothers. The deal was not to shed Joseph blood but to throw him in the pit. Being thrown in the pit is not a good thing but it kept him alive. As they were trying to figure out a lie of what they was going to tell their father about what happen to Joseph, they saw strangers the Ishmaelites coming. Then they decided to sell him as property to strangers so they did and gained 20 pieces of silver. After the Ishmaelites purchased him they journeyed with him to Egypt. After arriving with him in Egypt, the Ishmaelites gained a profit for selling him into slavery to an Officer of Pharaoh a Captain of the guards named Potiphar. The Lord was with Joseph so that he prospered, and he lived in the house of his Egyptian master. When his master saw that the Lord was with him and that the Lord gave him success in everything he did, Joseph found favor in his eyes and became his attendant. Potiphar put him in charge of his household, and he entrusted to his care everything he owned. From the time he put him in charge of his household and of all that he owned, the Lord blessed the household of the Egyptian because of Joseph. The blessing of the Lord was on everything Potiphar had, both in the house and in the field. So Potiphar left everything he had in Joseph's care; with Joseph in charge, he did not concern himself with anything except the food he ate.

NEXT, was when Potiphar, his master heard the story his wife had told him, saying, "This is how your slave treated me," he burned with anger. Joseph's master took him and put him in prison, the place where the king's prisoners were confined. But while Joseph was there in the prison, the Lord was with him; he showed him kindness and granted him favor in the eyes of the prison warden. So the warden put Joseph in charge of all those held in the prison, and he was made responsible for all that was done there. The warden paid no attention to anything under Joseph's care, because the Lord was with Joseph and gave him success in whatever he did.

NEXT, was when Pharaoh himself sent and called for Joseph. They quickly brought him from prison. Just imagined you're in prison serving your sentence. Thinking that you have been forgotten about and all of sudden you are rushed out because The President of the Country sent and called for you. They shaved Joseph, cleaned him and changed his clothes. From a slave in prisoner to now he standing in front of the Pharaoh and he say, I heard of you and the things you can do. Pharaoh said to Joseph, I heard that you can interpret dreams and went on to say, I had a dream. **Understand when you help others on the way, God will bless you all your days.** Just imagined, if Joseph didn't go through what he went through, would he had move in position of power? Joseph kept the momentum because he didn't delay his process. **By going through your process this will keep you when you reach the top**. Most people will not be able to hold their position because they didn't go all the way through their process. **No preparation to stay will cause you to go away**. When you're incomplete you can't finished the job because you're not fully developed into your position. To become developed into your position and take up residence you have to go through the process to affirm your being there.

19

ECONOMIC INVESTMENT PLAN

Joseph was thirty years of age when he was chosen to his position of authority. And with his support system, his wife by his side they conceived two sons. And through the conception of their sons it reminded him of what he had to endure to get chosen to his position and the blessings that come with what he had to go through.

In Genesis 41:51-52, And Joseph called the name of the firstborn Manasseh: For God said he, hath made me forget all my toil, and all my father's house. And the name of the second called he, Ephraim: For God hath caused me to be fruitful in the land of my affliction.

Joseph through Pharaoh's dream had put together a masterful plan that will save Egypt Economic System. Regardless, that he was in prison, he was in his rightful position to be chosen leader to rule. Don't downplay where you are. No place is lower then what Joseph been in; the pit, slavery and in prison. Be encouraged and know if you can look up you can get up. His Hardship became his Championship!

Joseph master plan was to save Egypt Economic System. He went all throughout Egypt, gathering and storing enormous amounts of grain from each city. He didn't go around spending just because he had it to spend. During his prosperous season he put back and saved because he knew it was going to come a time that the grain was going to run out according to Pharaoh's dream. Genesis 41:30-32 Seven years of great abundance are coming throughout the land of Egypt, but seven years of famine will follow them. Then all the abundance in Egypt will be forgotten, and the famine will ravage the land. The abundance in the land will not be remembered, because the famine that follows it will be so severe. The reason the dream was given to Pharaoh in two forms is that the matter has been firmly decided by God, and God will do it soon. During the seven years of abundance, Joseph stored up huge quantities of grain in each city from the fields surrounding them (Genesis 41:47-49).

Joseph saved Egypt and Canaan by selling the people grain during the 7 year famine. When the people had run out of money, Joseph bought their livestock. When they had run out of livestock he bought the land titles. . (Genesis 47:13-17) When the economy became bad, Joseph began to invest. The people that needed the money sold what they had. Joseph being a smart business men knew that he will gain a profit from his investment because God had reveal it to him in Pharoah's dream during the seven years of famine. Joseph bought up all the land in Egypt for Pharaoh. The priests did not have to sell their land as Pharaoh gave them a supply of food (Genesis 47:18-22).

Ecclesiastes 3:1 says, "To everything there is a season, and a time to every purpose under the heaven:"

We have to be responsible when it comes to our dreams because it's not going to take care of itself. Why spend all you have just because you have it. Why not spend a little but be like Joseph and put some a way for the future. You never know when the famine is going to come. It is better being safe than sorry. Cut back and invest in you. Don't touch it, let it build up. If you have a savings account let it draw interest. Every little bit counts. Better something then nothing. Especially, if you're living paycheck to paycheck, your famine will come when you get a pink slip. What will happen when your famine comes? And again we're back too "U", if you don't provide for your dreams who will? Who Can U Run To? You have all the resources you need to succeed. It doesn't have to take a lot. Use what you have. Look around and see what you have to work with. Don't be discouraged with what you don't have but be encouraged with what you do have. Everything begins with "U". **Once "U", know what it is that you want to do, you have to have a master plan to see it through.**

20

LIVING IN ABUNDANCE

When God begin to bless you, it's not only for you, but it's also for you to be a blessing to others. When God chose Joseph through his dream to rule over Egypt, it wasn't just to give him a position of authority. It was a set up for him to be blessing and to help those in need. That's why, it's imperative that you're not wasting time waiting for manna to drop from heaven. It's time for you to get up and make an effort to do something. When you take one step, God will use his servants to bless you. When God blesses you, can He trust you to be a blessing to others? Joseph was chosen because God trusted him to be obedient to what he called him to do. **Who better to trust to be a blessing to others than the person who's obedient to God?** It is evident when we look at Joseph life's journey and how he handled his personal affairs, as well as, how he took care of others property that God entrusted him and put him in charge. When the seven years of plenteousness, that was in the land of Egypt, were ended; and the seven years of dearth began to come, according as Joseph had said: and the dearth was in all lands; but in all the land of Egypt there was bread; and when all the land of Egypt was famished, the people cried to Pharaoh for bread: and Pharaoh said unto all the Egyptians, Go unto Joseph; what he said to you, do. And the famine was over all the face of the earth: And Joseph opened all the storehouses, and sold unto the Egyptians; and the famine waxed sore in the land of

Egypt. And all countries came into Egypt to Joseph for
to buy corn; because that the famine was so sore in all
lands.

Now when Joseph father Jacob heard that there
was corn in Egypt he sent all his son's Joseph brothers
except Benjamin to buy corn. When they arrived in
Egypt Joseph recognized them but they didn't
recognize Joseph. Joseph was reminded of the dreams
which he dreamed of them. The same dream the
brothers hated him for was this dream that will save
their lives and bless them. The dream was about Joseph
ruling over them. Even his father Jacob rebuked him
because such a dream that he will bow down to him.
Joseph brothers did bow down to him and was given
the opportunity to buy corn to take back to their father
Jacob and their family. The famine was sore in the land.
That it came to pass, when they had eaten up the corn
which they had brought out of Egypt, their father said
unto them, Go again, buy us some more food. When
the pantry and refrigerator becomes empty, it's time to
go grocery shopping. As they did, they went back to
Egypt to buy food. They had to go through some
obstacles before they could purchase food. In order for
them to purchase more food Joseph required that the
whole family be accounted for. The brothers had to
bring their father Jacob and their younger brother
Benjamin to Egypt. When Joseph revealed himself to
his brothers he could not refrain himself from crying.
The brothers were troubled at his presence. Joseph told
them do not be grieved, nor be angry with yourselves,
that you sold me into slavery: for God did send me
before you to preserve life. And God sent me before

you to preserve you posterity in the earth, and to save your lives by a great deliverance. So now it was not you that sent me here, but God: and he had made me a father to Pharaoh, and lord over his entire house, and a ruler throughout all the land of Egypt. God will cause your enemies to bless you even if the enemy is your family members. And Joseph said unto his brothers, and unto his father's house, I will go up, and show Pharaoh, and say unto him, my brothers and my father's house, which were in the land of Canaan, are come unto me. And Pharaoh said unto Joseph, your father and your brothers are come. The land of Egypt is before you, in the best of the land make your father and brother live; in the land of Goshen let them live; and if you know any men of activity among them, then make them rulers over my cattle. Then Joseph gave the people seed to sow the land. And the people said to Joseph you have saved our lives. And Joseph said unto them fear not: for am I in the place of God? **But as for you, you thought evil against me; but God meant it unto good, to bring pass, as it is this day, to save much people alive.**

21

LOST IT ALL BUT DIDN'T FALL

There may be many distressing circumstances we find ourselves in, and some of them may even be unjust, as were those in Joseph's life. However, as we learn from the account of Joseph's life, by remaining faithful and accepting that God is ultimately in charge, we can be confident that God will reward our faithfulness in the fullness of time.

Perhaps most profoundly, Joseph's story presents amazing insight into how God sovereignty works to overcome evil and bring about His plan. After all his ordeals, Joseph is able to see God's hand at work. As he reveals his identity to his brothers, Joseph speaks of their sin this way: "Do not be distressed and do not be angry with yourselves for selling me here, because it was to save lives that God sent me ahead of you. . . . It was not you who sent me here, but God" (Genesis 45:7-8). Later, Joseph again reassures his brothers, offering forgiveness and saying, "You intended to harm me, but God intended it for good"(Genesis 50:20). Man's most wicked intentions can never thwart the perfect plan of God.

Joel 2:25-26 And I will restore to you the years that the locust hath eaten, the cankerworm, and the caterpillar, and the palmerworm, my great army which I sent among you. And you shall eat in plenty, and be satisfied, and praise the name of the Lord your God that hath dealt wondrously with you: and my people shall never be ashamed.

There was this lady who lost it all but didn't fall. After 25 years of marriage out of nowhere her husband asked for a divorce because he met someone else. No warning that he was leaving his wife of 25 years and their two children. They were in the process of building a new home but after her husband had left it fell through because the bills were due. The wife and her children had nowhere to go, so they had to check in a motel. Barely making ends meet then their came defeat, when she got the call. The call was a blow because it was a termination from her job. No warning at all when she received this call. Fifteen years with this company and all she heard was you're no longer needed because it was your fault but no evidence of their plot; it sounds like foul play. Nevertheless, no time to complain because had to put food on the table, pay for transportation and had to provide shelter. The lady became homeless and without a job. Where does she go from here? The economy is bad and everyone is mad because they too are having it bad. So WHO CAN U RUN TO when everything else fails? It hurts because no green (money) will make you mean and when you lose hope it will also make you mope. As she looked in her children eyes, it makes her want to cry because she knew that they were confused. They went from living in a luxury home with their own rooms and a backyard with a swimming pool, to living out of the car and motel rooms. They were asking the question, mommy, why did daddy leave us? Question after question, she's doing everything possible to stay strong but deep inside she want to scream and cry. Haven't dealt with her pain of the divorce, she becomes numb to the thought of even going on, but those two pair of eyes that are depending on her. Her energy comes from her children and when she felt weak she's reminded of them and that's what makes her strong. No time for pity parties, she had to figure out a plan to move on. She's on her grind, flipping burgers, cleaning bathrooms, throwing newspapers and doing whatever it takes to carry on. Early morning rising and late nights is her schedule. She's the last one to go to sleep because she's crying and praying that her strength want fail. After all, she's doing it all. She's sacrificing and putting things on hold to make sure she's providing for her household. Encouraging herself day by day praying that God will bless what comes what may. Even not knowing what the next hour may bring, she's still hoping and dreaming that this too shall pass. Losing it all doesn't truly mean you lost it all. It's just **a setback to come back from the attack of lack**. She's still alive, she's still had her health, and she's still in her right mind. Even there were times she felt like she was going to lose her mind. She realizes a breakdown doesn't mean for her to stay down but it means she's exhausted all to begin and start anew. She didn't allow her life's ups and downs to keep her from turning it all around. She became responsible for her life, and the choices she made. She began to know and understand what was produced from her choices. She negated the downfalls and pitfalls by living life in abundance; living in abundance of love, joy, peace and happiness. Instead of her getting bitter she got better. Never in her life did she think she will be starting over again. Life had punched her by surprise. The punch intention was to KNOCK her OUT and keep her down; never to rise no more. But when she heard the countdown of her life slowly slipping away she began to "GET UP".

22

KNOCKOUT RESULTS INTO GETTING UP

When a boxer is in the ring fighting for the prize to win, they know they have to guard themselves from punches that are coming from all directions. Some punches will miss but you have those punches that will land. There is a punch that the fighter didn't see coming. Now this type of punch will knock the fighter off their feet and the taste out of their mouth. Breathless as the fighter lay flat on his back not knowing how to come back. The fighter vision is blurred and confused as where he is. The fighter heard voices in the background saying different things. One person was counting, many were shouting "GET UP" and the others were taunting saying you've been "KNOCKED OUT". With all the noise, the fighter start to understand what was going on. He understood the person counting was a countdown to his life, the next persons was cheering him on to get up and fight, and the last persons he heard was those who was laughing at him because he was lying on his back and couldn't get up because of the blow he was dealt. He knew time was running out because he heard 10, 9, 8 … He couldn't just lie on his back and throw in the towel because he's in pain. That would be the cowardly thing to do because he had sacrificed for this fight. He had done a lot of intensive training and preparing his mind for the unthinkable. There is no way he will allow a blow like this defeat what he work so hard to achieve. If he came this far in the fight no need of stopping in round five.

He decided to fight until all the rounds were completed. Seven more rounds to go in this particular fight, so he knew in order to make it to the twelfth round he had to get up. The countdown continues. Slowly but surely the fighter started to get up. Now he's on his knees. Then he put one foot forward followed by the other. Then with all his strength he stood up. Still feeling a little distraught from the punch he got in a protective position. He also began to bob and weave from the punches. Remember, just because you got up doesn't mean the punches going to stop being thrown. Gasping for air the fighter continues to fight his way through not letting it stop his momentum. As he walked forward, he threw a punch that ended that particular fight.

As the fighter was, so was the woman who got knocked out with the punch of life. This blow may have hit her where it hurts but the pain helped her to regain sight of her surroundings. She knew time waits for no one. She knew that it was no need of letting it keep her down. She started on her knees which is a posture of prayer. Then she put one foot forward which was followed by the other foot. When you pray you have to get up and give your prayer feet. Meaning you have to walk by faith. In the Book of James chapter 2 verse 26b, Faith without works is dead. When you pray, you can't stay where you are, you have to get up and continue in your faith knowing without a doubt that your prayer will be answered. When you get up off your knees from praying, your prayer continues. First Thessalonians chapter 5 verse 17 says, "Pray without ceasing." When you pray without ceasing you're continually listen to

God for your answer and direction on what to do next. As you're waiting for your prayers to be answered, you don't literally stop everything. You continue working on moving forward because this will position you to be where you need to be when your prayers are answered.

Proverbs 3:5-6 states "Trust in the Lord with all your heart; and lean not unto your own understanding. In all your ways acknowledge Him, and he shall direct your paths."

The woman was like Joseph. She didn't only just get up but she arose to the top. Now she's living in abundance of Love, Joy, Peace and Happiness. She remarried. She moved into a new home. Her children graduated high school and college. And her finances are blessed.

Proverbs 31:10-31,

[10] Who can find a virtuous woman? For her price is far above rubies.

[11] The heart of her husband doth safely trust in her, so that he shall have no need of spoil.

[12] She will do him good and not evil all the days of her life.

[13] She seeketh wool, and flax, and worketh willingly with her hands.

[14] She is like the merchants' ships; she bringeth her food from afar.

[15] She riseth also while it is yet night, and giveth meat to her household, and a portion to her maidens.

[16] She considereth a field, and buyeth it: with the fruit of her hands she planteth a vineyard.

[17] She girdeth her loins with strength, and strengtheneth her arms.

[18] She perceiveth that her merchandise is good: her candle goeth not out by night.

[19] She layeth her hands to the spindle, and her hands hold the distaff.

[20] She stretcheth out her hand to the poor; yea, she reacheth forth her hands to the needy.

[21] She is not afraid of the snow for her household: for all her household are clothed with scarlet.

[22] She maketh herself coverings of tapestry; her clothing is silk and purple.

[23] Her husband is known in the gates, when he sitteth among the elders of the land.

[24] She maketh fine linen, and selleth it; and delivereth girdles unto the merchant.

25 Strength and honour are her clothing; and she shall rejoice in time to come.

26 She openeth her mouth with wisdom; and in her tongue is the law of kindness.

27 She looketh well to the ways of her household, and eateth not the bread of idleness.

28 Her children arise up, and call her blessed; her husband also, and he praiseth her.

29 Many daughters have done virtuously, but thou excellest them all.

30 Favour is deceitful, and beauty is vain: but a woman that feareth the Lord, she shall be praised.

31 Give her of the fruit of her hands; and let her own works praise her in the gates.

23

AFFLICTED TO VICTORY

No matter what you're going through God will see you through.

Many are the afflictions of the righteous: but the Lord delivered them out of all their troubles. (Psalm 34:19)

Joseph was afflicted as many of you are. You may be afflicted with cancer, lupus, fibromyalgia, HIV, Parkinson, sickle cell, heart disease, shingles and etc. Be encouraged because God Knows and God Cares.

And behold, there was a woman who had a spirit of infirmity eighteen years, and was bowed together, and could in no wise lift up herself. And when Jesus saw her, he called her to him, and said unto her, Woman, you are loosed from your infirmity. And he laid his hands on her: and immediately she was made straight, and glorified God. (Luke13:11-13)

Behold, I am the LORD, the GOD of all flesh: is there anything too hard for me? (Jeremiah 32:27)

Things come to test us. Tests have a purpose. Tests are the process by which the genuineness of our faith is determined. Throughout this process, the quality of steadfast character is developed. We as humans undergo many tests throughout this life, as indeed all humans must, but we are also given a pattern to follow in handling them. It is hard enough to maintain a decent attitude when you are going through troubles that you know you brought on yourself. But what about things that are patently unfair? But when you do well and suffer for it, if you take it patiently, this is commendable before God. For to this you were called, because Christ also suffered for us, leaving us an example, that you should follow His steps. 'Who committed no sin, nor was guile found in His mouth'; who, when He was reviled, did not revile in return; when He suffered, He did not threaten, but committed Himself to Him who judges righteously" (1 Peter 2:19–23).

Let's briefly look at the Book of Job. The Patriarch Job is as an outstanding example of steadfast faith in the way he handled severe trials. The Book of Job is the story of a normal human being who is beset by misfortune and suffering. One of the most overwhelming things about a severe trial can be the sense of isolation. We want to make sure that God knows because when He finds out, surely He'll do something about it! In Job we are given a behind-the-scenes look at events of which Job was completely unaware.

God, however, was very much aware of Job and of the wholehearted obedience he sought to render. In fact, God Himself called Satan's attention to Job. Christ reminded His disciples in Luke 12:6–7 that God, who even takes detailed note of the sparrows, is much more deeply interested in the affairs of His own children. The Father is aware of everything about us down to the smallest detail. Even the hairs of our head are numbered.

When we are struck with personal tragedy or persecuted for obedience, we can be sure that God knows. This is vitally important to keep in mind to counteract the sense of isolation and loneliness that will often beset us at such times. "No one understands what I'm going through," we think. But Jesus Christ does. We have a faithful High Priest who was tested in all ways like us and is therefore able to empathize and give us the needed help (Hebrews 4:15–16).

Though Job could not begin to understand why all of these things were happening to him, he knew God was aware of it. He did not react, as Satan had predicted, by cursing God. Rather, Job told his wife, "Shall we indeed accept good from God, and shall we not accept adversity?" (Job 2:10). When we begin reading the book of Job we learn that, while God allowed Satan to afflict Job, He set limits beyond which the devil could not pass. From the start we know there are limits to Job's trial. He allowed Job to be personally stricken, but insisted that his life be spared. God has established the limits of our trial, but we just do not know what those limits are. Job was so certain of his innocence and of the injustice of his afflictions that for a long time he was unable to see beyond that. He tried to defend himself from the false conclusions of his friends and in so doing was unable to see areas of needed growth in his life. God has reasons for allowing whatever happens—though we are often at a loss to fathom what they are. In our trials and tests, James encourages us to ask God for wisdom (James 1:5). If we do so in faith, He will surely give it. Whatever the trial or test, there is always growth that can be achieved.

Even Jesus Christ Himself learned by the things He suffered (Hebrews 5:8). God wants us to grow. Therefore, we must undergo periodic pruning to stimulate that growth (John 15:2). Job was in despair. His whole life had been turned upside down. He had lost his wealth and his loved ones in a series of sudden calamities. Now his health was gone too. Why? Job was deeply frustrated because he could not make sense out of his trials. Yet in the depths of perplexity and despair he made one of the most profound declarations of faith recorded in the Bible: "Though He slay me, yet will I trust Him" (13:15). "All the days of my appointed time will I wait, till my change come (14:14 KJV).

It's easy to trust God when things are going the way we like them. When the world around us makes sense it is fairly easy to believe God is in charge. What about when things turn upside down and inside out? It is in the midst of such perplexity and anguish that faith in God is most needed. Job came to really know God deeply, not simply to know about Him. He became a far more humble and compassionate man as a result of what he went through. And God restored all back to Job; his health, his family, and his finances.

Third John verse 2 says Beloved I wish above all things that you may prosper and be in health, even as your soul prospered.

God has chosen you as he did Joseph and Job to be a blessing to those who are watching you. Your outcome will determine their becoming. So you can't allow the trial to overtake you and you sure can't give up. You have to be like Queen Esther in the Book of Esther; she saved a whole nation from being annihilated, as Joseph also saved his family and a nation of people from famine. So God trust "U"! So whatever is afflicting you know that it is a test to make you the best and to bless! Psalm 119:71 says, "It was good for me that I have been afflicted, that I might learn…"

24

GROWING UP: THE FALL OFF

As I grew up seeing a lot things and experiencing things that I didn't understand, I wondered was I suppose to experience certain things or even go through that. It wasn't until I was mature enough to understand why I went through some of the things I did. It was like Joseph, it was to position me where I am today. Not everything I experienced felt good because most of it was painful even to digest. It was a difficult journey to contend with. On my journey, I had to redirect my path because of the immature decisions I made. I believe **we are where we are because of the decisions we made**. Some decisions were good and some were bad. Most importantly, we have to learn from our bad decisions. I've learned when we know better, than we should do better. There is no need of staying mad at the bad choices made because this can be a set back to our WIP of "BECOMING".

Once upon a time, at a young age we may not have understood why people who called themselves our friends had stopped talking to us, when we didn't do anything to them. Not just associates but close friends like best friends that we called our sister and brother. Even our parents invited them in the family. They had the same access as though they were our real sister and brother. They knew all our secrets and bloopers that no one else will dare know. We entrusted them with our life. Then one day out of nowhere they stop speaking to us even stop returning our phone calls. We pondered of what we did wrong. We ask ourselves, did we say something to hurt their feelings? As far back as we can remember, we were always there for them, even when they called and needed someone to talk to. No matter what time it was, it could've been in the midnight hour, even then we will get out of our bed to go check on them. With no explanation the friendship was cut off. Yes, it might have hurt but we had to move on. In moving forward another incident happen when we heard of our friends and family having parties and events that we weren't invited too. Feeling left out we asked, why wasn't we invited? The answer we would get was we thought you wouldn't want to come. So you ask yourself, did I have something on me or was I wearing something that would indicate I didn't want to come? You say to yourself, I love to have fun too. I use to be the life of the party well I thought, anyway. It hurt to see everyone that you were cool with go and have fun without you. Being young and immature, you didn't know why they would treat you like a stranger. How dare them to treat you as if you never belonged. Confused and not knowing there was a reason that you were being stripped of "NOUN" that's persons, places and things.

In the Book of Genesis Chapter 37 Joseph wore a coat of many colors that symbolizes favoritism. **When you're favored by God you will be separated for preparation to be used by Him.** I didn't know at the time I was being separated from the "NOUN". Even though it hurt like a gut punch but it was for my good. I didn't understand why everyone at the time was dismissing themselves from my life even separated through death. I had made up in my mind at a young age I wasn't getting close to no one else because it was hurtful. I had decided if you weren't in my family or already my friend there was no getting in. The door was locked and my heart was closed. The things we say when we are young and immature to alleviate the pain.

First Corinthians 13:11 says, "When I was a child, I spoke as a child, I understood as a child: but when I became a man/woman, I put away childish things."

As I did because I no longer operate on a child way of doing things anymore that's when things started to fall off of me. I began to change. I know I wasn't the same. Was this the reason that my friends and family separated themselves because they identified the change in me? Was this the reason they no longer wanted me around in certain occasions? I began to understand that God was using them to separate from me because at the time I was too immature to do it myself. I wouldn't have let go but I would've tried to hang on to those who I was unequal yoke with. Not knowing the separation was necessary to propel me to my NEXT. If I wouldn't have been separated, it would have damaged me and kept me from my life journey that God had prepared for me. It wouldn't have just damaged me but it may have killed me. So in order to remove me from the "NOUN" God used those whom were close to me to separate from me. Sometime the pain is necessary to get us to move on. Even being in some relationships growing up I didn't know that **a broken heart can be a future**

blessing to a past messing. I used my broken heart experience to my advantage because no one wants to revisit that type of hurt. This was the ultimate pain of not turning back to that which hurts but to move forward to that which is great. **I learned through my pain to refrain from what caused the pain and to train for my gain.** Life lesson learned. We have to be cautious of whom we let in our life so they will not hinder our process of "BECOMING".

25

DEVELOPING: THE LAYOFF

When people began to separate themselves from me at first I didn't understand why. But when I understood why, my heart became merry.

Proverbs 3:13 Happy is the man that find wisdom, and the man that gets understanding.

Now understanding that everything that comes in my life isn't meant to stay. Some things, as well as, people are short term. Everything is not longevity. And just because its short term doesn't mean it's not significant. I believe all things have a purpose, even if we qualify it as good or bad. Remember, the cow manure that was mentioned earlier. As I began to get an understanding through my experiences, I realize it's developing me into my purpose. Each experience can be a teaching aid, if you're willing to learn from it. Use your experience to learn. My motto is, "There are two things we learn from others and that is, "What to do and What Not to do".

My separations not only come from persons but in this instance, separation comes through places. Remember, as mentioned earlier that a NOUN is termed as persons, places or things. Once upon a time, I was temporarily laid off of on a job. My employer told me that it shouldn't be no more than couple weeks then I will go back to work. During my layoff, I began to work for a temporary agency to keep my money coming in. During this period, I was in need of a car because my car needed major repairs which cost a lot of loot. So I went car shopping. Then sooner than later, I found the car that fit my needs. I made the down payment, did the paper work and closed the deal. The auto sales dealer gave me the keys to the car. Out the door I went to my new car. Smiling and looking cute at the same time. After my family heard I purchased a car they wanted to see it. So I showed the car to my family. They were happy for me. A week later of having my car I woke up one morning and I looked out the window, what did I see? My car was about to be towed away. All they told me was at the time, that we can allow you to get your items out of the car. So I called the dealership to ask why? And they said your employer said that you no longer worked at their establishment. WOW. So I called my employer and acquired about my job. Without notice I was terminated. It was a gut check and blow; No Job, No Money, and No Car. I not only felt hurt but I was embarrassed about people asking about what happen to my car. REPO: repossession is someone retrieving possession of something. Even though it hurt losing the car but it was for my good. I was released from a contract that wouldn't benefit me in the future. What looks good on the outside was a cover up; a lemon in the making. Most people get in lemon relationships with someone based upon how they look on outside or what they have. Not knowing at the time the persons have major issues and the things they possessed, possessed them because they can't make the payments. Stop trying to hold on to a lemon that you can't make lemonade from. It's time to go from lemons to lemonade.

Anyway, sometime later I was hired at another job with great benefits. Everything was going good and I had the opportunity of getting another car. My work performance landed me a promotion. Everything was back on track, my rent and my car payments were being paid on time. I was holding it down until, Oh my, what now? What is this a pink slip with my name on it? Hmmm, I thought this must be a mistake. Yep, here I go again, terminated without proof of what I was accused of doing. My termination had to do with absences based on a point system. There was a malfunction in the computer system which they refused to override because they said the computer doesn't lie. A company based on computer system, I had no choice but to pack my items and move on.

Now I began to think about what is this job thing about. I'm doing everything I suppose to be doing. I'm on time to work, never late from my breaks and my job performance is great. And the time I do have to take off from work it's due to sickness and doctor appointments. Not letting it get me down, I continue to grind because I had bills and they're not going to pay themselves. So I continue to search for employment. It didn't matter if I was qualified or not, I still submitted my resume. One night before bed I had a dream of the place I will be working in. I found it odd because I never thought I will be doing that type of work. But nevertheless, when I received the call to come for an interview I did. I believe if I hadn't had the dream I would've been hesitate about taken the position. Long story short, I got the job with excellent benefits. Oh my, I'm on the right road now. No worries and no complaints just on my grind and putting in my time. Big Money and I had No Worries!

26

LAY ASIDE EVERY WEIGHT

I went from separation from persons, places, to now things. While I was enjoying the fruit of my labor shopping and etc…I heard those four letters, "FAST". A fast is when you deny self of selfish desires. I also learned through fasting it positions us not to do our will but God's will be done in our lives. I had to fast a year from shopping. I could no longer use my money to buy clothes nor shoes but someone could buy it for me; I just couldn't hint and let them know I wanted that outfit nor those shoes. Now, if you love shoes, you know how I felt. It was hard at first but I made it through. When I was fasting from buying clothes and shoes, I was called to another fast the last 6 months, simultaneously, with the other fast. I had to fast from sweets and fried foods. Ok, this wouldn't have been such a problem for me but this is going into the fall season, where there are football parities, wings and things. Not only football season but my birthday is September 27th, the day my Aunt Juanita bakes me Chocolate on Chocolate cake, then theirs my Mom's Thanksgiving dinner, my BFF Christmas dinner and not to mention our family birthday bash. This wasn't good. I thought but who am I to be disobedient because God knows best. This was preparing me for where God was taking me, it taught me responsibility and it also disciplined me from me. I made my own money and I spent it the way I wanted to, until God loved me enough to call me to fasting. God was literary helping me to change from the inside out. It detoxified me. It cleansed my way of making decisions and taking responsibility of my economic system.

My job started to demand more of my time. Meaning more hours than usual I had to work. More hours means, more money. Before the fast it would've meant more money, more shopping. Working these extra hours, I began to get sick. I went to the doctor where they did blood work and ran test on me trying to find out what was causing me to pass out. My body began to feel fatigue, no energy. I began to look and feel like superman when he began to lose his powers; weakness from Kryptonite syndrome. The doctor couldn't find a diagnosis, but he did see it's something going on with me because it was evident on the outside in my appearance. So he prescribed me medication for energy in the day time and medication to slow me down at bedtime, so I could rest. This wasn't good because medication was making me worse then what I was. My energy was high and low, as though, I took an energy drink; crashing. When I first drank it, I had a burst of energy, than I began to slow down feeling exhausted and tired. I didn't want to lose my job, so I continue to drive 90 minutes each day; 45 minutes to work and 45 minutes back home. Several times I passed out while I was driving but it was the grace of God that I made it home safely. I was dedicated to my job. It didn't matter how I felt. I didn't want to take off work. My dedication led me to a promotion that I wasn't qualified for. I was so happy it was offered to me. Before I could accept the position, I looked at how it would interfere with me going to church on Sundays, mid-week Bible class and spending time with my family. I had to make a decision. I ask myself could my health uphold the weight that comes with this position. This position will also interfere with the plans God has for me. He had called me to be a Minister of the Gospel of Jesus Christ. So I had to turn down the position. Once I made the decision to turn down the promotion, God called me off the job. I asked, what I have to quit too; thinking about my bad experiences with my other jobs of being terminated. Now I'm on a job where my employer respects me, and offered me the supervisor position with an increase in pay. Hold up, I said. Then I asked the most important question, WHO'S GOING TO PAY MY BILLS? I HAD BILLS. And if I leave my job, the benefits are GONE too. My Faith was tested!

Also in Chapter 6 in the Book of Judges, Gideon faith was tested. He was fearful so he hesitated when God called him to GO. God sees us, not just how we were in the past or how we are at this moment, but also what He purposed us to become. Gideon was a weak man; that is how he saw himself. He was the least member of the smallest family in the smallest tribe. He was hiding out while treading grain so the Midianites wouldn't steal it. After this encounter with the Angel of the Lord, we see other evidences of how he viewed himself. When you do things in secret, it's evident that you're in hiding and don't want to be revealed. When God asked him to tear down some idols, he did it at night, when others wouldn't see him. He stayed in the house, while his father defended him. He asked for a sign (the fleece) not once, but twice. And God encouraged him by allowing him to overhear a dream of a Midianite soldier.

Yet, under God's direction, he led a troop of 300 men to victory over an army of 135,000. It did not matter what Gideon saw in himself; it mattered what God saw. Gideon, like you, is not an insignificant person. God created Gideon for a purpose and He created you for a purpose. And like Gideon, it may be your purpose for you to accomplish something much greater than you might imagine. Gideon was obedient to God's call in spite of his fear and doubt. He started out as a bitter and weak farmer, but was transformed into a warrior in a most unlikely fashion. He experienced a personal revival. Even though he was still fearful, he was willing to take a risk. Maybe he was so willing to take a risk because he had 32,000 men at his disposal. But God said "You have too many warriors and when they win they are going to think they did it all by themselves (Judges 7:2). So tell them that whoever is afraid can go home." So Gideon gets up makes the announcement and 22,000 men leave, just like that, leaving Gideon with 10,000 men (Judges 7:3). And God tells Gideon in Judges 7:4-8, The Lord spoke to Gideon again, "There are still too many men. Bring them down to the water and I will thin the ranks some more. When I say, 'This one should go with you,' pick him to go; when I say, 'This one should not go with you,' do not take him." So he brought the men down to the water. Then the Lord said to Gideon, "Separate those who lap the water as a dog laps from those who kneel to drink." Three hundred men lapped; the rest of the men kneeled to drink water. The Lord said to Gideon, "With the three hundred men who lapped I will deliver the whole army and I will hand Midian over to you. The rest of the men should go home." The men who were chosen took supplies and their trumpets. Gideon sent all the men of Israel back to their homes; he kept only three hundred men.

Judges 7:16 He divided the three hundred men into three units. He gave them all trumpets and empty jars with torches inside them. 7:17 He said to them, "Watch me and do as I do. Watch closely! I am going to the edge of the camp. Do as I do! 7:18 When, I and all who are with me blow our trumpets, you also blow your trumpets all around the camp.

They blew their trumpets and broke the jars they were carrying. In 7:20 all three units blew their trumpets and broke their jars. They held the torches in their left hand and the trumpets in their right. Then they yelled, "A sword for the Lord and for Gideon!" 7:21 they stood in order all around the camp. The whole army ran away; they shouted as they scrambled away. 7:22 When the three hundred men blew their trumpets, the Lord caused the Midianites to attack one another with their swords throughout the camp. God is looking for a Gideon today - men and women of faith, who are willing to step out and do great things.

I grew up a daughter of a Marine. I remember my father, Sgt. Eugene Pullen Jr. use to have a poster of Marines in his office that read, "Looking for a *Few Good Men*". I remember my pops saying it only takes a faithful few to get the job done! Jesus said, "For many are called but few are chosen."(Matthew 22:14) Those that are chosen are those who are willing and faithful to accomplish the task. They have decided to lay aside every weight NOUN (persons, places or things) that tries to hold them down. They have proceeded forward and pressing toward the mark of getting the job done!

God can use ordinary people to do extraordinary things. The steps of Gideon's victory are easy to trace: he had a promise to believe, an altar to build, a vessel to break, a lamp to burn, and a trumpet to blow. And God gave the victory! None of these things were that incredibly difficult. But Gideon did them in obedience and God blessed him. There are so many simple things you can do that God will bless. A small number with God can do much. Though He is not opposed to having many on His side, God loves to work through the few. You may be among the few in your company or on your ball team that has come out of the winepress to face the challenges of the open plains with the enemy nearby. Gideon and his small band of 300 men turned the tide. One can grow from doubt to great faith. Gideon did it and so can "U". Leaders should be courageous and examples for others to follow. Notice how so many rallied behind someone who was so courageous. Many people won't get involved unless someone more courageous proves the way.

27

BECOMING: THE PAYOFF

Hebrews 11:6, But without faith it is impossible to please him: for he that comes to God must believe that He is, and that He is a rewarder of them that diligently seek him.

After praying I had the faith to step away from my job. In my hands were bills but God in my heart. I reminded myself that God is Jehovah Jireh; a provider. And His word He promised never to leave me nor forsake me. And He will supply all my needs according to his riches and glory by Christ Jesus (Philippians 4:19). And He reminded me to take no thought for tomorrow because I have covered you. Sure enough in 2004 when God called me off my job I began to preach His Word. On June 6, 2004, I was licensed as a Minister of The Gospel of Jesus Christ by my Pastor and my Church. Then later in September 2007, I was ordained with the approval of my Church and a Committee Board of Pastors.

First Corinthians 15:58 says, "…Be ye steadfast, unmoveable, always abounding in the work of the Lord, forasmuch as ye know that your labour in not in vain in the Lord."

On my journey I use to wonder WHO CAN U RUN TO after everything else had failed? Yes, it starts with us but it ends with God. It starts with us making the decision to serve a wonderful and awesome God. I never would have made it without Him because He saw the best in me! When I heard people say, that I wasn't going to be nothing nor amount to anything. In Deuteronomy 28:13 "and the Lord shall make you the head, and not the tail; and you shall be above only, and not be beneath..." I was talked about by other ministers and pastors because of my gender as a female preacher. Galatians 3:28 "There is neither, Jew nor Greek, there is neither bond nor free, there is neither male nor female: for you are all one in Christ Jesus." The sad thing was most of the leaders were women who counted me out. Yes, it hurt because I expected them to mentor me. WHO CAN U RUN TO when others have failed you and don't understand you? The person to run to is the person who created you. So God created man in His own image, in the image of God created He him; male and female created He them. (Genesis 1:27) I had to live above my circumstances in order to stay on top of things that are trying to put me down. Regardless, of how I was treated, I knew that God had His hand on my life. I was used, abused, lied on, talked about, dogged out, forgotten, and looked over mostly because of my gender. I was also falsely accused, manipulated, deceived, stolen from, and etc. As Joseph was, so was I. I didn't let those things deter me of moving forward. I had **no time to dwell on the past because I knew that it wouldn't last**. I took it day by day. I had some hard times but God turned those times into good times. God knew the plans He had toward me because when I walked away from my job and into the ministry, I didn't have any money, **BUT GOD**. I didn't know where my next meal was going to come from, **BUT**

GOD. I didn't know how I was going to pay my bills, **BUT GOD**. No gas in my car, **BUT GOD**. I lived by FAITH and WALK with God. When God called me to do His Will and not my own, I've learned through faith that I was to serve Him and not money. Money is a current medium of exchange as a means of payment or a measure of value. It is limited to what it can do because God is our SOURCE.

There was a poor widow woman in First Kings 17. She was in want, and desolate. Even though she was lacking, God used her to bless the Prophet Elijah. It is God's way, and it is His glory, to make use of, and put honor upon, the weak and foolish things of the world. O woman, great was thy faith; one has not found the like, no not in Israel. She took the prophet's word that she should not lose by it. Believe in the Lord your God, so shall you be established; believe in his prophets, so shall you prosper (2Chronicles20:20c). Those who can venture upon the promise of God will make no difficulty to expose and empty their selves in his service, by giving him his part first. Luke 6:38 NLT, "Give, and you will receive. Your gift will return to you in full—pressed down, shaken together to make room for more, running over, and poured into your lap. The amount you give will determine the amount you get back." Surely the increase of this widow's faith, enabled her to deny herself, and to depend upon the Divine promise, was as great a miracle, as the increase of her meal and oil. Happy are all who can trust in God and keep the faith, against all odds. The poor widow gave the prophet her last meal; in recompense of it, she and her son did eat above two years, in a time of famine. To have food from God's special favour, and in such good company as Elijah, made it more than doubly sweet. It is promised to those who trust in God, that **they shall not be ashamed in the famine** but they shall be satisfied. When Jesus blessed the food, He fed over 5000 with five loaves and two fishes. And when they did all eat and were filled, they took up twelve baskets full (Matthew 14; Mark 6; John 6).

He will make provision for the vision. Everything He showed me as a youngster in visions/dreams is coming to past. Everything is working itself out for my good.

Romans 8:28, "And we know that all things work together for good to them that love God, to them who are the called according to His purpose."

Fasting humbled me to the point of transformation of not my will but God's will be done in my life.

Romans 12:2 And be not conformed to this world: but be ye transformed by the renewing of your mind, that you may prove what is that good, and acceptable, and perfect, will of God.

When I changed my mind, God helped me change my life. I was BECOMING into what God has purpose for me.

Jeremiah 1:5, "Before I formed you in the belly I knew you; and before you came out of the womb I sanctified you, and I ordained you…"

John 10:10b, Jesus said, "….I am come that you might have life, and that you might have it more abundantly."

First John 5:11-14, "And this is what God has testified: He has given us eternal life, and this life is in his Son. Whoever has the Son has life; whoever does not have God's Son does not have life. I have written this to you who believe in the name of the Son of God; so that you may know you have eternal life. And we are confident that he hears us whenever we ask for anything that pleases him."

The steps of a good man are ordered by the Lord: and he delighted in his ways (Psalm 37:23).

Joshua began life in Egypt as a slave, under cruel Egyptian taskmasters, but he rose to be the leader of Israel, through faithful obedience to God. Moses gave Hosea son of Nun his new name: Joshua (*Yeshua* in Hebrew), which means "the Lord is Salvation." This name selection was the first indicator that Joshua was a "type," or picture, of Jesus Christ, the Messiah. When **Moses** sent 12 spies to scout the land of **Canaan**, only Joshua and Caleb, son of Jephunneh, believed the Israelites could conquer the land with God's help. Angry, God sent the Jews to wander in the wilderness for 40 years until that unfaithful generation died. Of those spies, only Joshua and Caleb survived.

Before the Jews entered Canaan, Moses died and Joshua became his successor. Spies were sent into Jericho. **Rahab**, a prostitute, sheltered them and then helped them escape. They swore to protect Rahab and her family when their army invaded. To enter the land, the Jews had to cross the flooded Jordan River. When the priests and Levites carried the **Ark of the Covenant** into the river, the water stopped flowing. This miracle mirrored the one God had performed at the **Red Sea**.

Joshua followed God's strange instructions for the **battle of Jericho**. For six days the army marched around the city. On the seventh day, they marched seven times, shouted, and the walls fell down flat. The Israelites swarmed in, killing every living thing except Rahab and her family.

Because Joshua was obedient, God performed another miracle at the battle of Gibeon. He made the sun stand still in the sky for an entire day so the Israelites could wipe out their enemies completely. Under Joshua 's godly leadership, the Israelites conquered the land of Canaan. Joshua assigned a portion to each of the 12 tribes.

As God did for Joshua, so can He also do for you? In Joshua 1:3, "Every place that the sole of your foot shall tread upon, that I have given unto you..." When I decided turned my life totally over to God by the renewing of my mind. Things began to happen. The dreams began to turn into reality. What He had promised began to come to pass. Like a movie being advertised by showing previews of the coming attractions. So have God showed me through this book, it will no longer be a preview but what He had promise will come to pass. Dreams becoming Reality!

CONCLUSION:

TODAY IS THE DAY U RUN YOUR RACE AT YOUR PACE

The favor God gave Joseph was greater than anything he had ever known. Joseph had been through the extreme; he had experience the pit, slavery, and prison. But the depth of his past was an indication of the height of his future! Whatever you have been through in the past is the indication on how you will be blessed in the future. It's up to you to "GO" through without stopping. Leaving your past behind will bring you to your future blessings! Don't allow your "NOUN"; persons, places, nor things, hinder you from moving into your destiny. When you move, those coming behind you can move. As long as you remain in one place there is no space for them to embrace their race. You have occupied this space long enough, it's time to get up, move, and get out of the way so others can come up. Be an example, to those who look up to you. If you're always looking down, what will your children have to look forward too? It starts with you. They are watching you. If the space that you're now occupying has become crowded, it's time to move and get out of the way so you can allow others to grow and develop. **Lingering in one space will cause you to lose the race.** For instance, if you're in a race and all the runners are at the starting place preparing to run.

They're stretching their bodies and preparing to get on their blocks; as soon as they hear "Get on your Mark", they step into their blocks getting their feet in position. The runner blocks are there to help the runner to get a good start. It helps the runner at the start of the race to get a good push of momentum forward. The next thing they hear is, "GET SET". Now the runner positions their bodies to run the race. They're now waiting to hear the shot of the gun, which indicates to the runners to "GO". What if you get the okay to "GO" and you don't move? You're still at the starting place; in your blocks while the other runners have left their blocks and began their race. So instead of leaving the blocks, you're still trying to figure out how to start; while you're doing that, life is passing you by. Runner after Runner is passing you by. Race after race is being run. Everyone has a starting place. The purpose is to start and get in the race. Others are waiting on you to get out of the blocks so they can start their race. STOP HOLDING UP YOUR LIFE and STOP GETTING IN THE WAY OF THOSE WHO ARE TRYING TO START! Get out of the blocks and run. **Staying in your lane will keep you from running in vain.** Exercising your gifts/talents will keep you in shape to move forward in your race. **God will give you grace to embrace your race to help you keep your pace. Run at a pace that will help you win your race!**

"….let us lay aside every weight, and the sin which do so easily beset us, and let us run with patience the race that is set before us." (Hebrew 12:1b) The race is not to the swift, nor the battle to the strong but to the one that endures.

Second Timothy chapter 4 verse 7 "I have fought the good fight, I have finished my race, I have kept the faith."

GET ON YOUR MARK! GET SET! RUN! DON'T STOP UNTIL YOU REACH YOUR FINISH LINE OF LIFE!

ABOUT THE AUTHOR

Dr. Michelle J. Pullen is a woman that carries her own definition of love. Her unique smile and humoristic approach will penetrate the hearts of those near and far. The true doctrine resides in the bottom of this vessel and is handled with special care. She loves pouring out her "love" to those who will receive. She is a woman after God's own heart, who will only speak what God directs her to speak at any given opportunity.

Dr. Pullen is Licensed and Ordained Minister. Her mission is, "Perfecting the Saints to Affect the World…Ephesians 4:12". She has been serving in the magnitude of a Teacher, Preacher, Counselor, Conference Speaker, and Entrepreneur.

Dr. Pullen currently holds a degree in Business Management, a Bachelor of Theology, two Master Degrees in Theology and Biblical Studies, Doctorate of Divinity, and Ph.D., which she uses all for Kingdom Building.

For Booking Information Contact:
P.O. Box 2003, Hewitt, Texas 76643.
WhoCanURunTo@gmail.com

ABOUT THE AUTHOR

www.ingramcontent.com/pod-product-compliance
Lightning Source LLC
LaVergne TN
LVHW021504080426
835509LV00018B/2397